A Man Exact and Truthful

John Rae and the Northwest Passage

Also by John Wilson

SELECTED NOVELS

North with Franklin: The Lost Journals of James Fitzjames
Graves of Ice
Shot at Dawn
Lost Cause
The Ruined City
The Alchemist's Dream
Heretic: The Heretic's Secret book I
Quest: The Heretic's Secret book II
Rebirth: The Heretic's Secret book III
The Heretic's Secret (single volume edition)
Written in Blood: The Complete Desert Legends Trilogy

TALES OF WAR

Wings of War: Tales of War book 1
Dark Terror: Tales of War book 2
A Dangerous Game: Tales of War book 3

THE CAUGHT IN CONFLICT COLLECTION

Four Steps to Death
Germania
Where Soldiers Lie
Lost in Spain
And in the Morning
Flames of the Tiger
Flags of War
Battle Scars
Death on the River

SELECTED NON-FICTION

Lands of Lost Content: A Memoir
A Soldier's Sketchbook: The Illustrated First World War Diary of R.H Rabjohn
John Franklin: Traveller on Undiscovered Seas
Norman Bethune: A Life of Passionate Conviction

A Man Exact and Truthful

John Rae and the Northwest Passage

John Wilson

Illustrations by Liz Milkau

Library and Archives Canada Cataloguing in Publication

Wilson, John (John Alexander), 1951 -

A Man Exact and Truthful: John Rae and the Northwest Passage/John Wilson

ISBN (kindle) 978-1-990483-20-2
ISBN (paperback) 978-1-990483-19-6

A Man Exact and Truthful: John Rae and the Northwest Passage was first published as Discovering the Arctic: The Story of John Rae by Napoleon Publishing, 2003

Cover and interior design by John Wilson

For more information on the author and his books, visit:

http://www.johnwilsonauthor.com

John Rae was *"...a man exact and truthful and his methods of travel a generation ahead of his time...he...put into effect the only sound principle of the traveller—that of doing in Rome as the Romans do."*

Viljalmur Stefansson

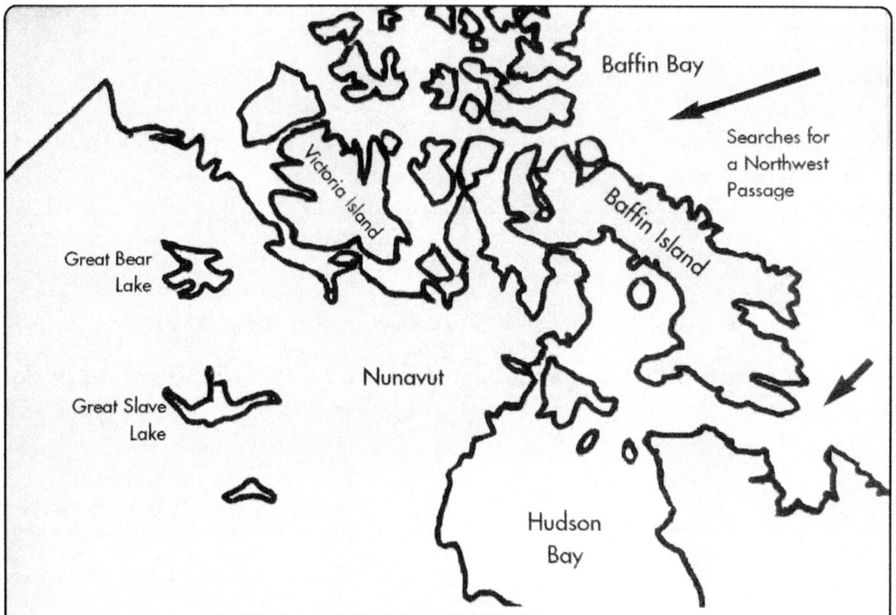

THE CANADIAN ARCTIC

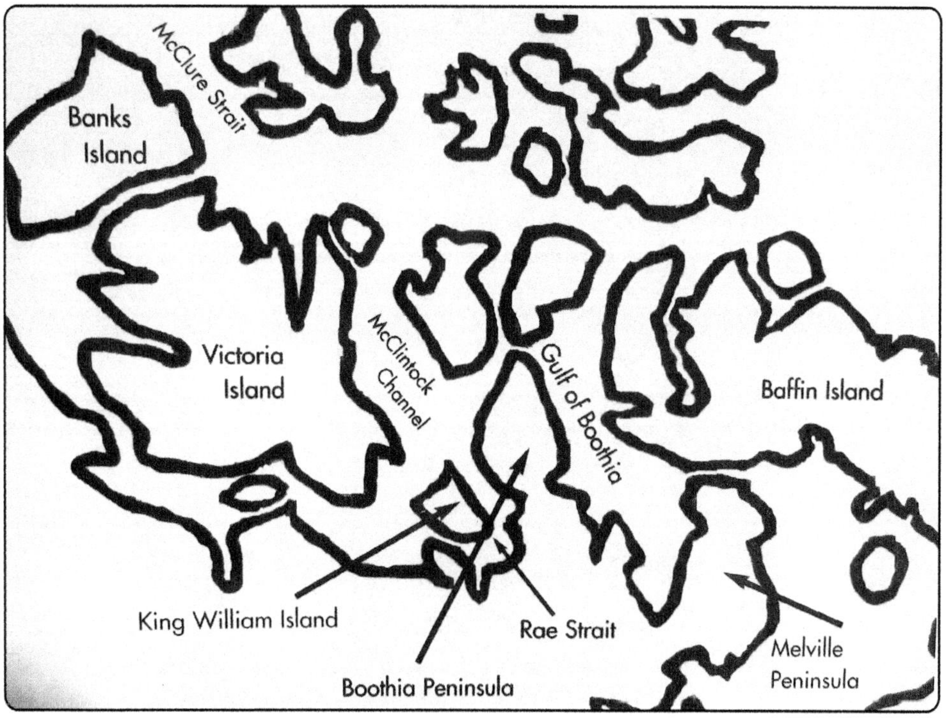

Into the Unknown

In voyaging west from Stromness, Rae was following in the footsteps of many famous men. Martin Frobisher, Henry Hudson, James Cook and Edward Parry had all used Login's Well in the centre of town to replenish their fresh water, and the sturdy Orkney men to replace missing crew members. Stromness was often the last sight of home for many years. For John Franklin and his crew, who passed through 12 years after John Rae, it was the last sight of home any of them would ever have.

On a blustery June day in 1833, the small sailing vessel, *Prince of Wales*, left Stromness harbour on Orkney, off the north coast of Scotland. On her deck stood a nineteen-year-old, newly-qualified doctor. As the ship began to roll in the choppy grey waters of the North Atlantic, he gazed westward as if trying to see what the future held.

Ahead was Cape Farewell, the southernmost tip of Greenland. From there, a ship could turn north into the frozen wastes of Baffin Bay, south to the fishing grounds of Newfoundland and Labrador, or west into the turbulent, ice-filled waters of Hudson Strait. The *Prince of Wales* would turn west through Hudson Strait into Hudson Bay, the gateway to the fur-rich but still largely unexplored interior of Canada.

There were opportunities for a young Orkney man prepared to work hard and learn—and John Rae was prepared to do both. But even in his wildest dreams, he could not have foreseen the dramatic successes and unjust disappointments that lay ahead.

Plans and Reality

Society in John Rae's day was rigid and unyielding by today's standards. There was a correct way of doing everything, from eating your supper to exploring the Arctic. It was not necessarily the best way, but it was the way that powerful people had decided things should be done. If you did things differently, even if your way was better, you ran the risk of being ignored—or worse, hated.

In 1833, John planned on spending a year working for the Hudson's Bay Company (HBC), getting some experience, and having a bit of an adventure. He would have been surprised to learn that it would be more than a quarter of a century before he returned to live in his homeland and a full 14 years before he even set foot there again.

In that time, Rae would walk, sledge or sail through thousands of kilometres of Canada's remote and inhospitable Arctic. He would learn to live like the Inuit, discover the tragic fate of Sir John Franklin's doomed expedition and stand on the shore of the fabled Northwest Passage.

Rae didn't know it, but he was on his way to becoming the most successful and resourceful Arctic traveller of his age. But he was also destined to feel the wrath of some of the most important people in England and to be passed over for the honours and recognition that fell to his less accomplished colleagues. It was a long, strange journey for a sensitive boy from remote Orkney.

John Rae

Only 15 kilometres (km) separate the 74 Orkney islands from the Scottish mainland, yet it is in many ways a different world. In John Rae's day, during the stormy winter weather, it could take weeks to make the voyage to or from the mainland.

Orkney has been inhabited for at least six thousand years. Ancient villages, rings of huge standing stones, and chambered tombs litter the treeless landscape as reminders of vanished people. For hundreds of years, Orkney was part of the Norse empire and home to some of the Viking raiders who terrorized much of Europe a thousand years ago. These rough seafarers treasured the remote land so much that Orkney only became part of Scotland in 1474.

The Ferrylouper

John Rae Sr., the explorer's father, was a "ferrylouper," or newcomer, to Orkney. He had been born and had grown up in southern Scotland, near Glasgow, but his energy and a desire to better himself led him to accept a position looking after the estate and 300 tenant farmers of Sir William Honyman.

Sir William was a powerful figure in Scotland, soon to take the title Lord Armadale, so becoming his overseer in Orkney gave John Sr. status and a relatively comfortable life. However, he never took it for granted and expected his seven surviving children to forge their own way in the world. Their challenge was to come to terms with the rugged moors and rocky coast of their island home, a process that instilled in the young John and his brothers and sisters a very independent spirit at an early age.

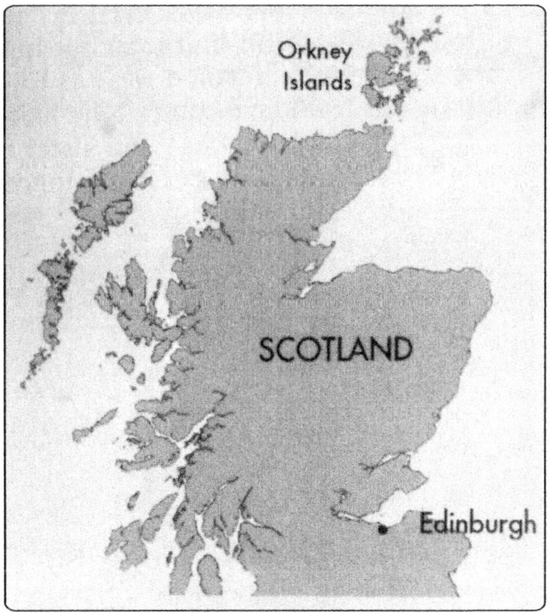

Orkney men, or Orcadians as they were known, were prized as employees by the Canadian fur companies. In 1800, the HBC employed 600 men, more than 450 of whom were Orcadians. These men from Orkney had several advantages in the eyes of the HBC. Accustomed to a hard life by the bleakness of their homeland, they were well suited to life in the Canadian wilderness. Unlike most labourers at that time, many of the Orcadians could read and write, suiting them to jobs as clerks and record-keepers. Finally, the Orcadian dialect, with its complex origins in Old Norse, Lowland Scots and English, made it relatively easy for the men to pick up the languages of the First Nations they were sent to trade with.

One HBC surveyor described Orcadians as, "the best men I ever saw...obliging, hardy, good canoe men."

Extra Responsibility

Despite the security of his position with Lord Armadale, John Rae Sr.'s drive would not let him rest. In 1819, he accepted the position of the HBC's chief representative in Orkney. This meant that he oversaw the needs of the two or three company ships that visited each summer on the way across the Atlantic.

John Sr. was also in charge of recruiting clerks, tradesmen and farmers for the HBC trading posts scattered across the Canadian wilderness. This part of his job was made easier by the HBC pay being twice what a farm labourer could earn at home. It also meant that he could find work for his sons. William and Richard sailed west as HBC clerks in 1827 and 1830 and young John as a ship's surgeon in 1833. Thomas and sister Marion followed later.

John Rae certainly inherited his father's drive, but John Sr.'s position allowed him to express that drive in ways neither could foresee.

Stromness harbour in Orkney

Birth

John Rae would have been born in one of the upstairs bedrooms of the Hall of Clestrain. There would likely not have been a doctor present, but Mrs. Rae would have been assisted by a local midwife.

In 1813, babies were born at home. This was fine for rich families who had spare rooms, servants and hygienic surroundings. It was a much greater problem for poor families who were crammed into dirty, tiny dwellings. Many babies got sick and died within the first year of life, because the world they came into was too dirty and crowded.

The cry of the newborn baby echoed through the solid stone house across the bay from Stromness, stopping the children in their tracks. They had been busy helping fetch hot water and linen, but mostly they had been told to keep out of the way of all the serious adult activity. Now it was different. That cry meant that they had a new brother or sister, and they crowded around the bedroom door, eager for a first glimpse.

John Rae joined his three brothers and two sisters on 30 September 1813 in the family home—the Hall of Clestrain. It was an old laird's (or landlord's) house and was suitably imposing for the Rae family's social position on the island. But none of that mattered to the children that day as they eagerly welcomed the new family member. It mattered even less to baby John, but it would as he grew and learned of this strange world surrounding him.

The Hall of Clestrain

Home Life

As the sixth child in a lively and energetic family, young John was teased a lot. In later life, he remembered that "sensitiveness and credulity" were two of his weaknesses. He could not "imagine or understand anyone telling untruth", especially for anything as unimportant as a joke, so he was constantly being tricked and having practical jokes played on him. He seems to have borne these teasings well, and never complained about his siblings. In fact, being the butt of practical jokes may have fitted him well to the rough and tumble humour of the isolated HBC posts where he was to spend much of his adult life.

John Rae Sr. was stern with his children. He expected them to look after themselves and not to bother him with petty requests. At dinner he would make everyone around the long table bow their heads and give thanks to a strict God for the bounty He had laid before them. John Sr. must have seemed a severe and distant person to a child. Young John's mother, on the other hand, was much gentler. The children probably went to her if they had a problem that appeared too petty to bother their father with. At dinner, she would concern herself more with ensuring that the younger children managed to get enough to eat as they competed with their older and hungrier brothers and sisters.

John Rae took characteristics from both his parents. His father gave him his self-sufficiency and his hardy character. His mother encouraged his open-mindedness and the concern he felt for the men who accompanied him on his expeditions.

A Famous Visitor

John Rae Sr. was important enough when young John was only a year old to have the famous novelist Sir Walter Scott visit him. Scott was researching his novel, *The Pirate*, and stayed at the Hall of Clestrain for some time in 1814. John claimed to remember him travelling to visit the ancient cathedral at Kirkwall and the even more ancient standing stones that were scattered across the Orkney landscape. Scott enjoyed his visit and gathered a lot of background information for his novel. In fact, two of the characters in it, Brenda and Minna, are based on John Rae's two older sisters.

In his diary of the visit, Scott compliments the Rae farm on being well-tended and with a good breed of horses. He also describes the life of the tenant farmers for whom John Sr. was responsible. Mostly they lived in small one or two room crofts built of stone and sod. The walls rarely had windows and usually there was only a hole in the roof to let out the heavy smoke from the peat fires. Most tenant families grew potatoes and barley, and some better-off crofters kept a few cattle or sheep that would share the shelter of the house in cold weather. Food was supplemented by hunting seals, birds and the occasional whale, and by fishing. Even so families went hungry in many years, and crop diseases such as the potato blight of the 1840s could produce real famine.

St. Magnus Cathedral, Kirkwall

The Hunter

Twelve-year-old John could barely lift the old flintlock musket his father had given him. How could he possibly shoot anything with this? Then he had an idea. Going around the farm, he busily created holes in the dry stone walls. In these he could rest the heavy gun and bag an impressive total of small game. Rabbits, ducks, plover, heron and curlews all fell to his rapidly improving aim.

John was a solitary child, and from a very early age he enjoyed spending long hours hiking over the moors, scrambling over rocks, climbing cliffs, riding, fishing and hunting. As he grew, John took to tramping over the local moors with the gun and his faithful dog, Carlo. There he would hunt grouse and often proudly returned home with enough game for the family supper.

In the early 19th century, getting food for the family was much more complex than today. There was no local grocery store where anything you might need could be put in a cart and taken home. People who lived in the country tried to be as self-sufficient as possible. In summer, they grew vegetables, and those not used were preserved for the winter. In the autumn, wild fruit and berries were collected and bottled for later use. Chickens, cows, goats and sheep provided eggs, milk, cheese and meat, and this was supplemented by hunting and fishing. Some staples such as flour, sugar and salt had to be bought in year-round, and what you did not grow yourself, you could buy in season at the local market. It was not unusual for a boy like John to grow up with a much greater sense of self-sufficiency than a boy today. Given what he was to do with his life, this was just as well.

Boating

A yawl is a small sailing vessel with two masts—the main mast, near the front of the boat and a shorter mizzen mast at the back. The jib sail is usually triangular and runs from the mainmast to the bow. The mainsail hangs on the mainmast and the mizzen sail is attached to the mizzenmast. To sail a yawl solo, as John Rae did, the sailor must know exactly what each sail and each combination of sails will do. It is a complicated business and requires a lot of practice.

John's father gave him and his brothers two boats, which were theirs as long as they looked after them. One was a small rowboat that was good for fishing near the shore or getting to and from the other boat. The larger boat was called the *Brenda* and was an eighteen foot long yawl. The *Brenda* was stable and fast, and the boys had great fun sailing her. As the youngest of her crew, John began with the simplest of tasks, in charge of the jib sheet, the small sail at the very front of the vessel. However, he soon progressed to the more complex sails aft and in no time was sailing the *Brenda* solo.

The Rae brothers used to challenge the town boys from Stromness to races and would occasionally take on the pilot boats whose job it was to guide ships through the tricky passages between the Islands. The pilot boats were very fast and the men who sailed them very experienced. In calm weather, the boys in the *Brenda* could not beat them. But when the water was rough and the wind squally, the *Brenda* was more manoeuverable and often won.

A yawl

In Britain, in the early 19th century, education was voluntary. What this meant was that if your parents were rich, you were given an education, either at a private school or, as John Rae was, through tutors. At the other end of the scale, churches provided some free schooling to the poorest children. However the bulk of the population had little if any formal education.

This was a problem, because life was becoming much more complicated as the industrial revolution progressed and an ability to read and write became, as the HBC found when hiring its clerks, increasingly important. But things happened slowly and it was not until 1880, when John Rae was an old man, that the British Government made elementary education compulsory for all children.

Education

All the Rae children were educated at home by a succession of tutors who came and lived with the family. This gave John's education flexibility that allowed him plenty of time for hunting and boating, but the standard of the education depended very much on the tutor. A good one could give a splendid and broad ranging education, but a poor one would be terrible. Rae remembered one tutor who kept pet eagles. Since these birds needed a constant supply of small birds for food, John was kept busy catching the eagles' supper.

In later life, John regretted that he had not gone to a grammar school with other boys his own age. However, his education, including the hunting, fishing and boating, could hardly have been better designed to fit him for the life he chose in Canada.

Medical School

In the 1830s, Edinburgh, dominated then as now by the outline of its famous castle, was a bustling city of 160,000 people. Its school of medicine was famous although it had a reputation for being politically radical.

By the age of 16, John Rae felt that Orkney had taught him all it could. He wanted to see the wider world, but he was not yet ready to go as far as the Canadian wilderness. Medicine interested him, probably in part because with medical qualifications you could travel wherever you wanted and still find work, this would not have been the case if John had followed his father into farming.

At first John thought of going to London to study but then he discovered that he would not be allowed to graduate before he was twenty-years-old. The Royal College of Surgeons (RCS) in Edinburgh did not have such a regulation, so John went there.

He spent four winters in Edinburgh in his own words "plodding through the various courses of study" and engaging in snowball fights with the boys from the town. In later life, that was all he claimed to remember from his time there. Nevertheless, in April 1833, at the age of 19 and after a rigorous oral exam, John Rae qualified as a doctor.

Edinburgh

Fulfilling a Dream

Rupert's Land, as much of North America was known in 1833, was the sole preserve of a single company. The HBC had been exploiting the wilderness that so attracted John Rae since the *Nonsuch* returned from Hudson Bay in 1669 with the first cargo of furs. Since then the company had, with the help of the local First Nations, been industriously harvesting beaver, otter, wolverine, fox, bear, marten, lynx and wolf pelts. Originally given all the lands that drained into Hudson Bay, the takeover of the rival North West Company in 1821 had expanded the company's land far to the west and north and there was continuous pressure to go ever further to see new stocks of the precious beaver skins.

At 19, John Rae was of average height and of a light build. He had a strength, wiriness and stamina that had been built through the rugged pursuits of his childhood, and a sharp, open and enquiring mind. He was also now a qualified doctor. John Rae was ready for the larger world.

While most of Rae's fellow doctors were seeking positions in medical practices either close to home or in Edinburgh, Rae was casting his gaze wider. Since boyhood he had watched the men his father had recruited, including two of his brothers, set off westward into the rugged landscape of North America to explore and exploit the wild rivers and dark forests and seek their fortune. This was the life John wanted, and that was why he took the job of ship's surgeon on the *Prince of Wales* in June 1833.

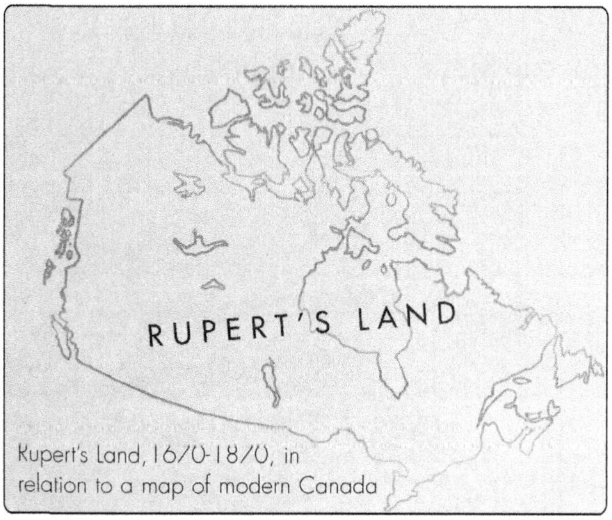

Rupert's Land, 1670-1870, in relation to a map of modern Canada

Fever Ship

The *Prince of Wales* was a barque, much bigger than Rae's beloved *Brenda*. It was a sixty-year-old, three-masted ship of 400 tons. *The Prince of Wales* was broad across, her sides were built of two metre thick oak and her bow reinforced with iron to protect her from pack ice. She was typical of the working ships that ploughed back and forth across the Atlantic every season, taking supplies west in the spring and furs back east in the autumn.

The *Prince of Wales* was fully loaded with everything from muskets and fishhooks to sealing wax and kettles. The food supplies included salt meat, flour, cheese, lemons, peas, spices and alcohol. John also saw live chickens, sheep and pigs.

John's first job as ship's surgeon was difficult. Although Rae had an individual cabin and ate at the Captain's table, not everyone on board was so lucky. Thirty-five Orcadians, setting out to help move the HBC furs across Canada, lived between decks in an evil-smelling, unlit, stuffy space only 1.5 metres high. They slept on boards or hammocks and ate salt beef and pork. Many suffered from seasickness. Even worse, almost as soon as the voyage began, typhoid fever broke out. For two weeks, John spent all his time ministering to the sick below decks. At the end of it, he was exhausted—but not one man died under his care.

After the typhoid outbreak, John spent his spare time learning about this unfamiliar ship, clambering about the rigging pestering the sailors to teach him the knots of their trade. He was fascinated by everything and filed all he learned away in his inquisitive brain. Much of it would prove useful later in his life, when he had no one but himself to rely on.

A four masted barque

The Voyage West

Early in July, as the *Prince of Wales* and her companion vessel, the *Prince Rupert,* entered Hudson Strait, John saw his first iceberg. As he wrote later, he was impressed by its "beauty and purity, vastness and variety," but unfortunately, the ice in Hudson Strait was more than just these pretty cathedrals of glittering ice. Before they had gone far, both ships were held fast in thick pack ice.

For two weeks, the ships sat, two kilometres apart, and John's only entertainment was the walk over the ice between them. The break up of the ice was marked by the arrival of several Inuit who busily began to trade for the knives, needles, axes and beads that had been brought for this purpose. In exchange, the Inuit gave seal oil and walrus ivory.

The inquisitive Rae examined the strangers closely, the beginnings of a process that would eventually allow him to live almost as efficiently as they did in their harsh Arctic home.

The Inuit who lived on the shores of Hudson Strait were familiar with the HBC ships that passed every year. They had seen them come and go with the open water since the *Nonsuch* had passed that way in 1668. Perhaps they told stories of even earlier encounters. The first European to make contact with the Inuit of Hudson Strait was Martin Frobisher in 1578, when he sailed about 300 kilometres along the strait in error, thinking it was Frobisher Bay. In 1610, Henry Hudson had some dealings with the Inuit of the area, and several of his mutinous crew were killed in an encounter with them in 1611. By John Rae's day, the Inuit and the HBC men had settled into a regular pattern of trade.

Games on the ice

Moose Factory

As soon as the two HBC ships entered Hudson Bay, they separated. The *Prince Rupert* headed west for York Factory, and the *Prince of Wales* sailed south into James Bay and Moose Factory. There, as the ship was emptied of supplies and loaded with furs, John Rae examined everything he could and tried to make himself as useful as possible.

His activities were noticed by the chief factor, John George McTavish, who invited Rae to remain as the factory doctor. Rae was tempted, but he had promised his mother that he would return that year. Accepting McTavish's gift of a birch bark canoe, and after only seventeen days on the soil of Rupert's Land, John Rae embarked for home.

John Rae was greatly impressed by the French-speaking voyageurs he met at Moose Factory. They were vibrant, loud, cheerful and brightly dressed. More importantly, their clothes were perfectly suited to the life they led, from their soft knee-length moccasins to their deerskin jackets and wide hats. Rae noticed how their dress contrasted with the much less practical suits and jackets worn by the HBC officers. Rae was unusual for his time in that he was flexible in his attitudes and would always select something based on practicality rather than fashion or style.

A voyageur

Delayed

When the *Prince of Wales* reached Hudson Strait on the return voyage, she found the *Prince Rupert* already there, facing a solid barrier of pack ice. After days of battering the ice, trying to force a way through, the two captains gave up. The *Prince Rupert* sailed west to Churchill to winter and the *Prince of Wales*, weighed down with 60-70 centimetres of ice on her decks, struggled south to an abandoned post on Charlton Island in James Bay. John Rae would not be allowed to leave Rupert's Land as easily as he had hoped.

Conditions in Hudson Strait are notoriously uncertain. Martin Frobisher found it foggy but calm in 1578, but when it was first recognized by John Davis in 1587, the ice was rushing through so ferociously that Davis did not enter and called it the Furious Overfall. Henry Hudson took almost 6 weeks to struggle through to Hudson Bay in 1610, and John Rae's experience showed that, even in the larger ships of two hundred years later, it was still a stretch of water to be reckoned with.

A ship trapped in the ice

Winter

Scurvy was a major killer of sailors for hundreds of years. It is caused by a lack of vitamin C, which in the days before vitamin pills, was only found in fresh food. Fresh fruit, vegetables and meat could prevent scurvy, but they were not available on long ocean voyages or during the winter in places like Charlton Island. Rae didn't know it but cranberries are rich in vitamin C, which is why feeding it to the sailors cured scurvy.

As the winter temperatures plummeted on Charlton Island, the men shivered in their makeshift shelters around their inefficient stoves. The cargo of furs was safely stored, but things were not going well. Some of the sailors had loose teeth, bleeding gums and blackened lips. They had scurvy and it was Rae's responsibility to cure them.

In 1833, the causes of scurvy were still unknown, but Rae speculated that it was a lack of something in fresh food. He hunted as much game as he could and tried boiling spruce shoots, but the situation continued to worsen. Many sailors could barely crawl. One man's teeth became so loose that he swallowed two of them in his sleep. Eventually, Rae had to watch helplessly as the Captain and the Chief Mate died.

Not until the spring thaw exposed some cranberries could Rae cure the sick. It was a harsh introduction to medicine in the New World.

Alcohol

In Rae's day, people commonly drank large amounts of strong liquor. Sailors were given large drinks of rum every day, and HBC men were given brandy. It was a sign of Rae's strength of character that he could resist the temptations all around him.

Rae suspected that the Captain and Chief Mate had died so quickly partly because they were already weak from drinking too much. Rae later described the mate's death as particularly unpleasant. "His mouth and tongue were black; his saliva was black as night, his limbs all purple, and…terribly wasted." The poor man also smelled so bad that Rae was the only one who would approach to wash and feed him.

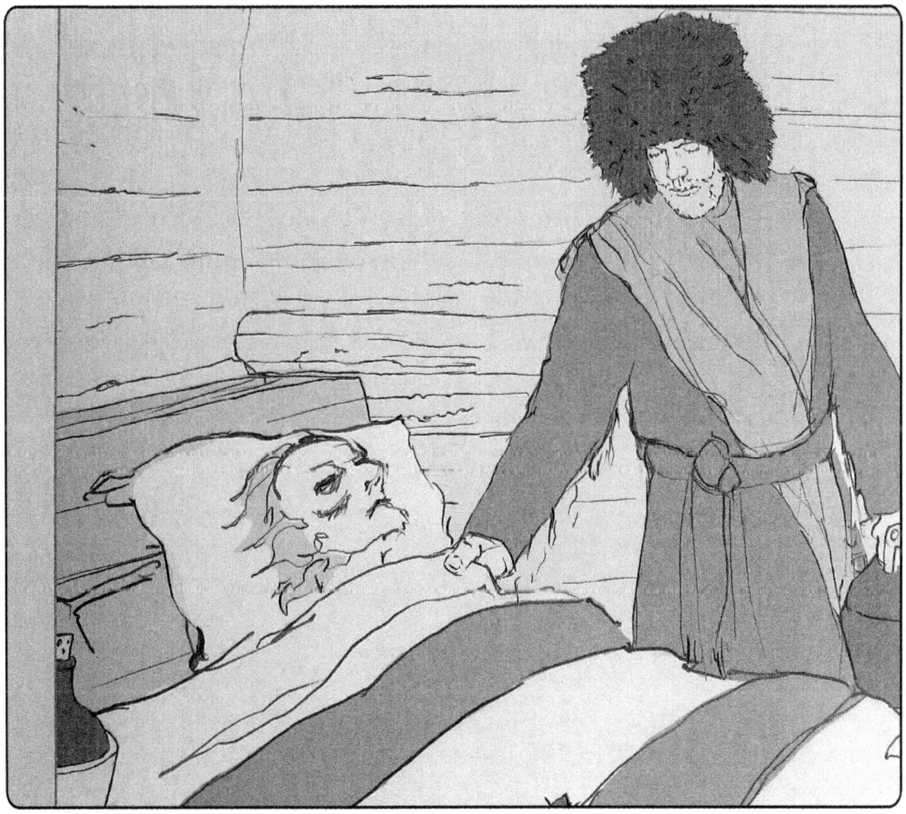

If alcohol had contributed to this horrible death, then Rae would have little to do with it. For the rest of the winter he abstained, and his only complaint was toothache.

For the rest of his life, Rae drank very little. He would have a glass of wine at a celebration, but nothing more.

Relief

With the arrival of spring, the hunting improved, and the ice melted. The ever inquisitive Rae took his birch bark canoe and went on a four day circumnavigation of the island. He left a novice canoer but returned determined to become an expert.

In mid-July, the *Prince of Wales* was refloated, reloaded with furs and sailed the 100 km to Moose Factory. There, Rae discovered that McTavish had written to his family on Orkney saying that he wanted to hire their son. He offered Rae the post of clerk and surgeon. Rae rejected the post of clerk as too dull but agreed to stay for at least two years as surgeon. Rae had learned a lot in the previous year, but his life was at a crossroads and his serious apprenticeship was about to begin. On August 12 1834 he watched the *Prince of Wales* begin the long journey home without him.

Moose Factory had been a trading post and fort since 1673. It had been captured by the French in 1686 and destroyed by fire in 1735, but it was always rebuilt. Situated on an island twenty kilometres from the mouth of the Moose River, the post was thirty days by canoe from Montréal.

The fort consisted of a sprawling two story building surrounding an open square. Inside were living quarters, a trading post, surgery and offices. Nearby were the dining hall and storeroom, and McTavish's comfortable two-storey house. Smaller cottages housed the married staff, church, workshops and a large hall where the single men lived. By the water, squat warehouses stored the precious bundles of furs awaiting the summer arrival of the ships from home. Although surrounded by sparsely inhabited wilderness, life at Moose Factory was relatively civilized.

Moose Factory in the 19th century

Christmas

Huge logs crackled in the vast fireplace. Dancing flames lit the decorated tree, wreaths and streamers.

Tables groaned with wild meat and fish, plum puddings and port, wine and brandy. The air was loud with jokes, toasts and stories. This was Christmas dinner in the hall at Moose Factory.

Eventually, everyone staggered over to the Bachelors' Hall, where the regular employees, swollen to nearly 200 with local trappers and First Nations people, danced to fiddles, spoons and drums and sang and shouted in Scots Gaelic, English, French and Cree. It was a wild time, filled with energy and fun, and this was just the beginning. The celebrations lasted a whole week.

Rae joined in all the celebrations, dancing late into the night with the best of them. But he never forgot the man who died so horribly on Charlton Island and limited himself to a single glass of wine with his Christmas dinner.

Wilderness Doctor

John Rae was only twenty-one when he was thrown into looking after the medical needs of the HBC staff of Moose Factory and a large number of Métis and Cree who lived nearby. Mostly he had to deal with rheumatism and chest complaints, caused by living in the harsh climate, and with axe or gunpowder accidents.

Much of the time there was not a lot to do, so Rae took on other duties to combat the boredom. He supervised the shipping of supplies to distant posts, an important job because if anything vital was forgotten or damaged in transit, it could mean the difference between life and death in the wilderness. Rae was also in charge of preparing the bales of furs for the shipment in the autumn.

Rae's first year at Moose Factory was marred by news that John Sr. had died at the age of sixty-two in October 1834. In 1827, Rae's parents had moved to The Haven outside Stromness where his mother, Margaret, lived on alone for more than 20 years.

The canoe landing strip at Moose Factory

Although Rae was a good doctor, there were limitations on what he could do. Medical knowledge in the 1830s was primitive by today's standards. For example, wounds caused by a slipped axe or the careless firing of a musket often became infected. There were no antibiotics, so the only solution to prevent the spread of infection was to cut off the infected limb. This was a brutal procedure, as there were also no anaesthetics in Rae's day. If you needed a leg or an arm cut off, your friends would give you some brandy, place some leather between your teeth so you wouldn't scream or bite your tongue off, then hold you down on a table for the doctor work as fast as possible. With luck, you fainted.

The Lifting Trick

Strength was needed in the fur trade both for moving supplies and canoes and for shipping the precious furs themselves. The furs were packed into bundles, the small, fine skins on the inside wrapped in the coarse, large skins on the outside. The bundles were then compressed into a hard rectangle and bound with leather thongs. Workers were expected to handle these heavy bundles with ease. A bonus was that, if you ran out of food in the wilderness, you could unwrap the furs, boil the pack cords and eat them in a kind of gluey soup.

Many of the HBC men took great pride in their physical strength, carrying two bales of fur, each weighing 41 kilograms (kg), at a time over rugged river portages. While Rae could not better these feats of brute strength, he used his intelligence to compete.

Stored in the trading post at Moose Factory were awkwardly shaped kegs of lead musket shot. These weighed nearly 150 kg and were usually stored on a shelf almost a metre off the floor. Rae and the storeman developed a trick to twisting and lifting these cumbersome loads into place. Rae, not a large man himself, would ask a particularly muscular man to lift one of the shot kegs into place. Not knowing the trick, thc man would fail. Rae would then appear surprised, smile, and with apparent ease twist and lift the keg onto the shelf. Rae was not a braggart or a show-off, but he enjoyed a good joke, and he was very competitive.

Learning

Rae's greatest talent was snow shoeing. He learned it making long winter trips to visit sick patients, and he could undertake extraordinary journeys with ease. He could travel 120 km in 24 hours, even with stops to brew tea. On one occasion he realized that he had forgotten to give a letter to the express mail. Knowing that the mail carriers would camp about 40 km away he set out at nine p.m. on a clear night. He reached the astonished men's camp at three a.m., breakfasted with them and returned to the fort the same day, bagging 28 grouse on the way back.

John Rae never thought the worse of anyone because of what they looked like or where they came from. The only thing that mattered to him was efficiency —could a man do what he said he could and what he needed to do to survive? In an age when many Englishman looked down upon the First Nations of North America and regarded them as savages and little better than animals, Rae appreciated the skills of the local people, skills that he would have to learn if he wanted to live in this new land as comfortably as the native inhabitants did.

One of Rae's closest friends in his Moose Factory years was a Cree called George Rivers. The two men hunted continuously, and Rivers taught Rae how to trap, camp, canoe and snowshoe properly. He taught Rae such important techniques as removing the gullet from slaughtered caribou to stop the meat going bad and how to save the animal's blood in a sack made from turning the stomach inside out. Added to what he had learned in his childhood and his natural hardiness, these lessons turned Rae into a master of life in the wilderness.

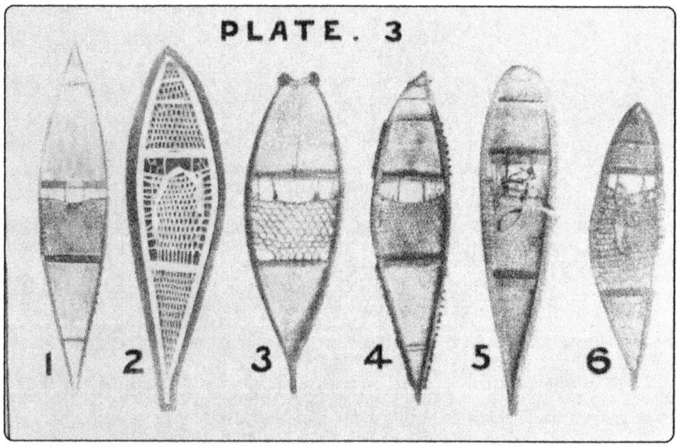

Learning from Women

The HBC men were lonely in the wilderness, and many of them married local First Nations women. This had the practical advantages of easing the loneliness and of giving new employees fresh out from Britain a crash course in wilderness survival. The marriage links formed were also an advantage in trade, forming a link between the two very different cultures that had only the trapping and shipping of furs in common.

Many of the marriages lasted for life and were based on true respect and love. Others were regarded as conveniences, and the First Nations wives were cruelly dumped when the HBC man returned home or brought a European bride back across the Atlantic.

This was a subject not much written about in the documents of the time, but it is certain that Rae formed several relationships with First Nations women. However, he never took the step of establishing a marriage.

In an age when women were dismissed as second-class citizens, Rae's attitudes were ahead of his time. John Rae appreciated the value of the skills exhibited by the Cree women who lived around Moose Factory. The women were seamstresses and were skilled at making efficient clothes from hides. This was a skill that Rae would need if he was to live off the land, and he learned it eagerly. From the women, he probably also learned how to snare small animals, how to prepare furs for trade, and how to chew tough moose hide so that it could be worked into clothing and footwear.

The Cree women were also the artists of their people and produced beautiful decorated beadwork on belts, bags and clothing. Rae appreciated the beauty of this work and built up a large collection that is now in the National Museum of Scotland in Edinburgh.

First Nations beadwork on a pouch

An Adventure

Rae's endurance was remarkable. He cheerfully suffered freezing temperatures and exhausting conditions that reduced younger men to quivering wrecks. Whether this was due only to his training in Orkney or whether he was physically more adapted to endure cold and privation is unknown. What is certain is that, even in a time when life was much harder than today, Rae was exceptional.

On one occasion, when George Rivers was unavailable, Rae went on a hunting trip with an inexperienced companion. From the very beginning, things began to go wrong. As the pair camped on a low island in a river, a violent storm broke. The river rose, swamping the island, and the two men had to take to the canoe. In the total darkness, amid crashing waves, Rae navigated them to some willow trees on another island. There, with the rain turning to snow, they huddled in the canoe as the raging river rose to within half a metre of the treetops. Even above the noise of the river, Rae could hear the teeth of his companion chattering, and his shivering shook the entire canoe.

At dawn, the river fell, and Rae, bundling his companion in his own blanket, left him and waded through the freezing water to hunt. He returned with some geese, found some driftwood and cooked a hot breakfast. Then with his companion still helpless with cold and fear and with his own wet clothes frozen stiff, Rae paddled 14 km against the river current.

Undoubtedly, Rae saved his companion's life, but he never boasted about it. He would simply shrug and said that the young man was not as used to the work as he was. Rae did, however, tend to go hunting on his own after this experience.

In John Rae's day, large freight canoes were the way the furs got from the wilderness to the shipping points of Moose and York Factory. They were constructed of birch bark, which made them light flexible and easy to repair, and crewed by voyageurs. These men were incredibly tough and proud of it. They could paddle hard all day and trot over long portages with 80 kg on their backs. To fuel these feats, the men would consume 4 kg of meat per day. No wonder they had a reputation for partying hard whenever they found themselves with some free time.

A Competition

Sir George Simpson, the governor of the HBC, travelled about his domain in a large canoe paddled by an elite crew of Iroquois trained to maintain 60 paddle strokes per minute. On one of his visit to Moose Factory, Simpson boasted about how his paddlers had beaten a small rowboat on Lake Winnipeg. Rae quietly observed that the rowboat must have been badly handled. He went on to state a rowboat with a crew of trained Orcadians could beat a canoe any day. A bet was born between the two competitive Scotsmen, and Rae set about supervising the construction of a small, six oared vessel that he named the *Brenda* after the boat of his childhood. He trained the crew hard and, when Governor Simpson arrived in the summer of 1843, all was ready for the great race.

On the morning of the race, the betting was heavy. A gunshot signalled the start of a 10 km course around the island on which Moose Factory sits. Everyone turned out to watch, and many were amazed to see the *Brenda* arrive back well before the canoe. Simpson was disappointed, but Rae had the sense not to boast about his achievement.

The Northwest Passage

When, more than 400 years ago, the first English explorers went looking for a route around the top of America, they were doing it for a specific reason. Frobisher, Drake, Hudson, Baffin and others were looking for a short route to the Spice Islands of Indonesia. In the 16th century, nutmeg, cloves and pepper were worth more than gold. On top of that, only one out of three ships that went looking for them by the old route around Africa made it home. If you could discover a shorter, safer route, you would become very wealthy and famous.

Unfortunately, by the 1630s, it was clear that there is no easy route. The issue was ignored for 200 years.

In the 1840s, the British Government felt that the Northwest Passage, which had eluded explorers since the 16th century, was within reach. One more expedition would do it. But who would command it? The government looked around. Eventually, their gaze landed on a man who had already mapped much of Canada's Arctic coast. True, at almost 60 years of age, he was a bit old to go gallivanting off to the Arctic, but it was said that he would "die of disappointment" if not allowed to go. In any case, no one expected any serious difficulties on the expedition. In the spring of 1845, command of the greatest Arctic expedition ever put together was given to Sir John Franklin.

Sir John Franklin

The 19th century British explorers, led by William Parry, John and James Ross, and Franklin were not looking for spices. Their search was for scientific knowledge. Discovering the Northwest Passage would be a great achievement, but it was an end in itself, much like the later searches for the North and South Poles. The similarity was that, if you failed in 1845, you were just as doomed as those who failed in 1611.

Sir George Simpson

Simpson and Dease

The HBC charter stated that the company had a duty to seek the fabled Northwest Passage. That duty had been mostly ignored, but there was pressure from England to map Canada's Arctic coast. Between 1837 and 1839, two HBC men, Thomas Simpson, the cousin of Sir George, and William Dease, had mapped a large stretch of Canada's northern coast by canoe. Thomas Simpson wanted to go back and complete the job but the following year he died in mysterious circumstances. The work was left unfinished. Sir George Simpson was looking for someone to continue his cousin's work. Knowing Rae's reputation on snowshoes and having seen his skill with a boat, Sir George was convinced he'd found his man. Swearing Rae to secrecy, Sir George asked him to prepare an exploration plan and come to Lachine near Montréal to present it.

To Montreal and Back

One of the major problems arctic explorers had was knowing where they were. Close to the Magnetic North Pole, their compasses were useless. Atmospheric refraction made the sun appear higher in the sky than it was, so readings commonly put explorers many km away from their actual location. Hours of complex readings and calculations were needed to determine, even approximately, where one was. But it was vital work. There was no point in going if you didn't know where you were when you got there.

John Rae spent his 30th birthday in 1843, paddling up the Abitibi River. He portaged over to the Ottawa River and then travelled by coach to Hamilton, where he spent time with his older brother Richard and his younger brother Thomas, who ran a dry goods store there.

Rae spent Christmas at Simpson's stone mansion in Lachine, visited nearby Montreal, then snowshoed the almost 1,000 km back to Moose Factory. There, Simpson sent Rae a detailed outline of the proposed Arctic adventure. It was Rae's plan, but the arrogant Sir George, who was known as the Little Emperor, worded it as if it were his own idea. One a good suggestion was that Rae learn how to operate navigational instruments so that he could determine his position in the Arctic. Over the course of the next two years, Rae did just that.

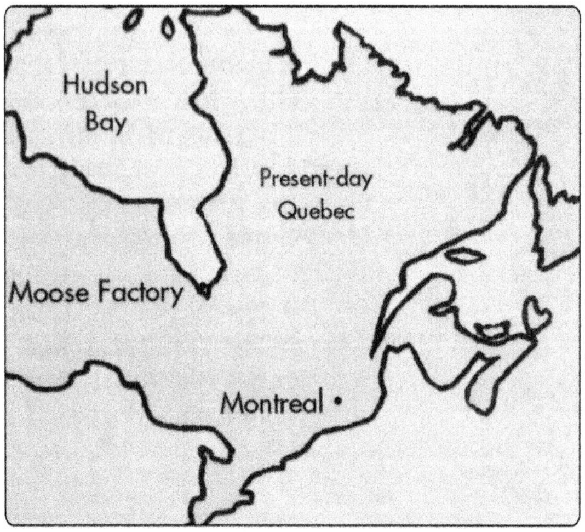

Franklin Sets Out

As John Rae prepared himself for his first expedition, across the world in England, Sir John Franklin was also ready. On Monday the 19th of May, 1845, his two ships the *Erebus* and the *Terror*, lifted anchor in the Thames River. With Sir John were 128 crew and enough supplies to last three years. Most people thought a single year would be enough. A few pessimists believe that two or three years might be necessary, but no one suspected the terrible disaster that lay ahead. A disaster that would pull John Rae in and determine the course of his life.

Sir John Franklin's ships setting off from London.

Learning to be an Explorer

For two years, Rae criss-crossed eastern Canada learning his new trade. No one gave his new venture much chance of success. Even Rae's old friend McTavish advised him to take as few men as possible to the Arctic, since none of them would ever be coming back.

The novelist Robert Ballantyne was more optimistic. He met Rae in the wilderness and was impressed by his intellect, "animal spirits" and "energetic character". Ballantyne felt that, if it were possible, Rae would succeed.

In the autumn of 1845, Rae arrived at York Factory on the western shore of Hudson Bay to find two boats waiting for him. These he christened the *North Pole* and *Magnet* and, in what was becoming a habit, challenged a local ship's captain to a race. Rae won easily and when the captain complained that it was because Rae had the better of the two boats, Rae swapped boats and won the second race.

A High and a Low

Rae's winter preparations were brightened by the presence at York Factory of remarkable lady named Letitia Hargrave, with whom he developed a close friendship. This happy time was marred by the news that his older brother William had committed suicide in California. William had worked for the HBC since 1827, but had become mixed up in revolutions after he was made chief trader in California. Problems with his marriage also contributed to his tragic death.

William's death hit John hard. After all, William had been the older brother that John admired and whom he had followed to seek his fortune in Canada. But there was little time for mourning. Spring would arrive soon and John had to be ready to head north.

Letitia Hargrave was the same age as John Rae. In 1840, she married James Hargrave and accompanied him to York Factory. For ten years, she wrote letters home to her mother in Scotland and became one of the very few people to record what life was like in those days for a woman in the wilderness. Letitia noted that the "state of society seems shocking," but was pleased with a good size house and piano, "a very fine one and the handsomest I ever saw."

In 1850, James was transferred to Sault Ste Marie, where Letitia died suddenly of cholera in 1854.

As Rae set off in the spring of 1846, far to the north, John Franklin and his men were preparing to leave their camp at Beechey Island, where they had spent a comfortable first winter. Franklin had shown there was no way through to the west or north and was ready to head south and west down the strait he had discovered, Peel Sound. The only blot had been the deaths of three of his men, but they had been sick for sometime and should never have come on the voyage in the first place. All in all, things were going very well for Sir John and his crews.

Heading North

On June 12, 1846, Rae told six Scotsmen, two French Canadians, one Métis and one Cree, "tomorrow we depart on the adventure of our lives." Then they set to packing the two boats. They took muskets, pemmican (a mixture of meat and animal fat packed into bags), a fishing net, oil lamps and stoves, four windows and an inflatable rubber boat. Next morning a salute of cannon fire and cheers accompanied the eleven men as they set off on their journey.

The expedition was planned to last fifteen months, yet they took only food enough for three. All the men were picked for their expertise, and this would be the first Arctic expedition to live off the land. It was a revolutionary concept, one that John Franklin could not understand.

Typically, a pemmican recipe might contain:

4 pounds dried caribou or moose meat
3 pounds Saskatoon berries
2 pounds lard
Salt to taste

The food provided energy and nourishment without needing to be kept cold.

Winter

Rae and his party sailed north to Repulse Bay, where they left one boat before dragging the other overland to explore Committee Bay. In August he returned to Repulse Bay to do something no European had ever done before—rely on his own skills to survive a winter in the high Arctic.

Many years later, this was all that remained of Rae's 1846/7 winter quarters.

The first thing Rae did was a mistake—he built a stone house. The walls were more than a half metre thick, there was a door of wood and deerskin, and three of the windows he had brought were set into the walls. But there were problems; the house was large, and stone is not a good insulator. As winter set in, it became very cold inside the house. Anything that got wet froze solid. In contrast, Rae noticed that Inuit camped nearby built snow houses that were warm and cosy inside, despite having no iron stove. Rae taught himself how to build snow houses and, by early December, he had constructed four joined by tunnels. The rest of the winter would be much more comfortable.

Weathering the Storms

Rae recorded how his party went about setting up camp when they were travelling. "Our usual mode of preparing lodgings for the night was as follows: as soon as we had selected a spot for our snow house, our Esquimaux, assisted by one or more of the men, commenced cutting out blocks of snow. When a sufficient number of these had been raised, the builder commenced his work, his assistant supplying him with material. A good roomy dwelling was thus raised in an hour."

As the temperature dipped below -40° C and the boats were covered with four metres of snow, Rae passed the time in his warm igloo reading Shakespeare. When the weather permitted, the men played soccer outside and, as spring approached, built two sleds with iron runners for exploration. Although Rae didn't realize it at the time, this was another mistake.

When he began travelling in the spring, Rae hired an Inuit man and his sled to transport supplies. The competitive Rae was mortified to see the man speed ahead with a heavier load than the European sleds were carrying. Rae discovered that the Inuit coated his sled runners with a mixture of moss and wet snow. This helped the runners glide more easily over the snow. Rae copied him and was soon speeding over the landscape.

In 1847, things were not going well for Franklin's expedition. After sailing down Peel Sound in the summer of 1846, Franklin's ships had become stuck in the ice north of King William Island, some 250 km west of where Rae was exploring.

The winter of 1846/47 passed successfully, and a sledging party from Franklin's ships could leave a note in May 1847 that ended "All Well". It would be the last time anybody could say that. On June 11 1847, as Rae settled comfortably back into his camp at Repulse Bay to await breakup of the ice so he could sail south, Sir John Franklin died.

In August, as Rae arrived back at Churchill with food to spare, Franklin's men realized that the ice was not going to release them that year and they were facing another desperate, hungry winter far from comfort or help.

Spring Journeys

Travelling over the mountains of sea ice was exhausting work. First there was a hard climb up one side, then there was the giddy slide down the other. The slide often ended in such a chaos of arms, legs and equipment that the men had to be dug out. As the spring sun grew stronger, Rae faced different problems. Often his team had to either wallow in waist-deep snow or slosh through freezing salt water. Rae began travelling at night and camping for the day before the sun melted the surface snow.

Rae persevered and completed two epic journeys around the shores of the south end of the Gulf of Boothia. In addition to adding hundreds of km of previously unexplored Arctic coast to the maps, he joined this work to what was already known proving that Boothia was a peninsula, not an island, and that there was no Northwest Passage this way.

Despite the gruelling work, when Rae returned south to Churchill in July 1847, people were amazed at how healthy he and his men looked. Rae had a surprise of his own. At York Factory he learned that a British naval expedition had recently passed through searching for Sir John Franklin, of whom nothing had been heard.

One opinion in Britain in 1847 was that if uneducated natives could survive in the Arctic, then it would be easy for civilized men to do the same. The stupid assertion must have made John Rae shake his head. He knew first-hand how difficult it was to hunt caribou and muskox, what incredibly specialized skills and patience were necessary to kill and retrieve seals, and how little game there was in the Arctic at certain times of the year. Rae had thrived with a small party of highly skilled men. He must've been very worried about how much the ten times larger and vastly less experienced party under Franklin would have been suffering at that very moment.

Home

Sir George Simpson had not expected Rae to complete his tasks nearly as fast as he had. He therefore offered the explorer free time to do what he wished before his duties would require him in 1848. Simpson assumed that there would only be enough time for a trip within Canada. Rae had other ideas. He had not seen Scotland for 14 years, so, on September 24 1847, only three weeks after his return from the north, Rae boarded a ship for home.

In Britain, Rae visited his mother and other relatives in Orkney. He also met Sir John Richardson, a famous naturalist and Franklin's companion on two expeditions to the Arctic in the 1820s. Richardson wanted to go looking for his old friend, and he wanted Rae to come with him. The whole of Britain was becoming obsessed with finding Franklin, so how could Rae resist? On March 25th, 1848, after writing to inform Simpson of his plans, Rae set off from Liverpool for the Arctic.

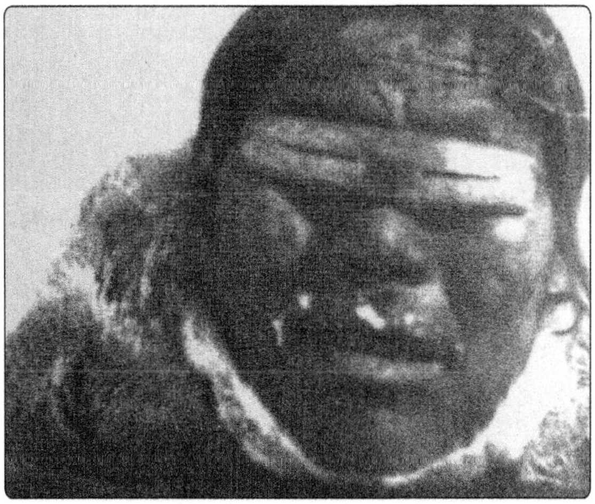

The Inuit had adapted to their environment in ways the Europeans did not understand. Here a man wears sun goggles (made of wood, bone, ivory or leather) that cut down the sun's glare and helped prevent snow blindness

Lost

As Rae and Richardson were searching the Arctic coast, far to the east, the Franklin expedition was falling apart. In April with food running low, with scurvy and a host of other illnesses breaking out, with 24 men already dead, and with no sign of rescue, the survivors abandoned their ships and headed south. They were a pitiful sight dragging their sleds across the frozen wastes until, one by one they dropped dead.

Franklin's ship, the *Terror*, in the ice.

Some made it to richer hunting grounds, some returned to the ships, and a few probably survived for a year or two more, but 1848 saw the end of the Franklin expedition and all its high hopes.

The 1848 Search—part 1

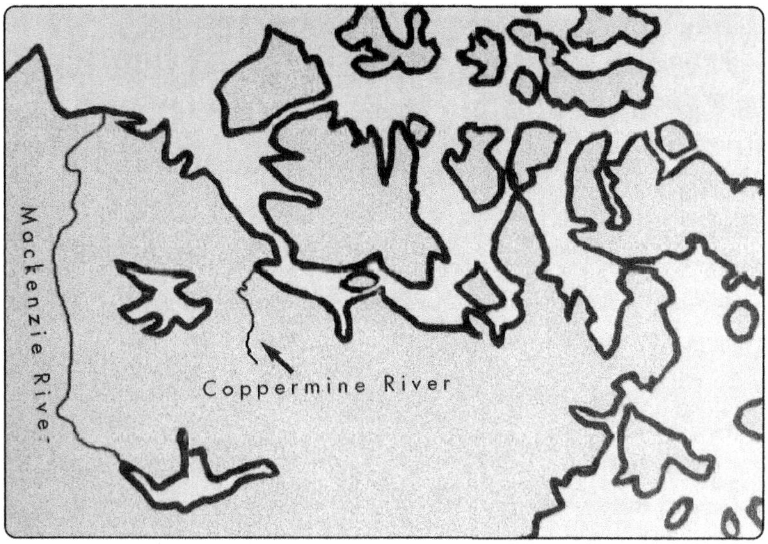

In 1848, Rae and Richardson travelled by canoe and sledge across North America, then by boat down the Mackenzie River and along the Arctic coast, and on foot back up the Coppermine River. It was an immense journey undertaken at frantic speed. To simply reach the Arctic coast, Rae and Richardson travelled almost 6000 km in only 90 days. For all their effort, they found no trace of Franklin or his men.

For Rae it was a frustrating experience travelling with British Navy men rather than the voyageurs, Inuit or Orcadians he had come to respect. The British sailors were not suitably clothed, could not hunt, could not carry anything close to the weight that a voyageur or Rae himself could carry with ease, and were not hardened to the harsh climate.

Mackenzie River in 1901

The 1848 Search—part 2

The British sailors' ignorance was due to arrogance. Franklin suffered from it too. In his book about his 1821 explorations along the Arctic coast, Franklin ridiculed his voyageurs' concerns about the unsuitability of their canoes for Arctic travel, the lack of food and the hazards of travel over the Barren Lands. Franklin wrote this passage after the voyageurs had been proven right on all three points, and more than half this party had died as a result.

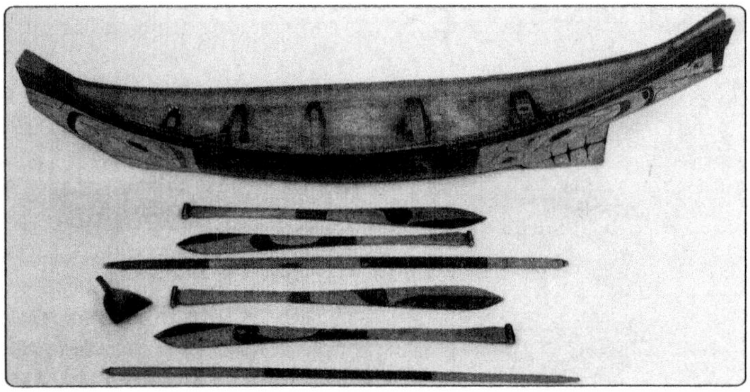

In September, as the group was slogging back along the Coppermine River, Rae, who was used to being wet through when travelling and hunting at this time of year, was amazed to overhear a serviceman complain at the possibility of getting rheumatism because he'd got his feet wet. Rae was also furious when he discovered that a vital block of pemmican had been abandoned as being too heavy to carry. He berated the sailors and threatened that he, Richardson, and his Inuit interpreter and hunting companion, Albert One-Eye, would abandon the men to their fate in the wilderness. No one left any pemmican behind after that.

Disappointment and Tragedy

With mounting horror, Rae watched as his boat broke free from the haulers on the bank of the Coppermine River and was swept down the rapids at Bloody Falls. Bravely, Albert One-Eye leapt on board to try and secure it. Rae breathed a sigh of relief as the boat and its single occupant were pulled into an eddy by the far bank. But the whirlpool was too strong. The battered boat was dragged under. Albert leapt for the shore but slipped on the wet rocks and vanished beneath the swirling water. He was never seen again.

Bloody Falls

The tragedy was a hideous end to a bad season. For weeks Rae and his five hand-picked men had sat frustrated on the Arctic coast, unable to go farther through the churning ice floes. Whenever open water appeared, Rae had tried to continue, but he was always driven back by the dangerous conditions. Eventually he had to give up and retreat south. And now this.

Rae was distraught. Albert had been a splendid travelling companion. He was the only man who died on any of Rae's expeditions, but that didn't make his loss any easier. Rae sat on a log and wept for the courageous and cheerful young man who had been his friend.

Hopes Dashed

Jane Franklin

John Rae spent the winter of 1849/50 at Fort Confidence on Great Bear Lake attending to HBC business. He was tired and upset at Albert's death. He had accomplished much, and the fact that he was not searching in the right place for Franklin was hardly his fault. He was also lonely. At 35, he was thinking of returning home, finding a wife, and settling down to raise a family, and had already written to Sir George Simpson requesting leave. But in late June 1850, while Rae was transporting furs along with Mackenzie River, an express canoe reached him and handed him three letters.

The first letter was from Simpson. No one had yet found any word of Franklin, and Rae was to continue his search next season. The second letter was from Franklin's wife, Jane, begging him to find her husband. The third letter was from Sir Francis Beaufort at the Admiralty outlining other expeditions that would support Rae's efforts.

Rae could hardly turn down such powerful pressure, even though, after five years with no word, there could be no hope of good news about Franklin's fate. Continuing on his way, a weary Rae began planning yet another trip to the inhospitable Arctic.

The remains of some of Franklin's men on King William Island

A Tale of Horror

If any of Franklin's men were still alive in 1850, they too had probably sunk to the horrific experience of Pambrun's companion. As Rae himself was later to hear, the Inuit told stories of finding camps of dead sailors and evidence of cannibalism.

More recently, the bones of some of Franklin's sailors have revealed traces of knife marks that could only have come from cutting up the bodies for the meat. It was a horror that no one liked to talk about, but it was a reality in the harsh wilderness that Rae was about to return to.

John Rae's low mood in the spring of 1850 may have been made worse by a story he had heard from two HBC clerks only a few weeks before. The station at Pelly Banks, more than 1600 km away, had burned down the previous November. After building a rough shelter, the man in charge, Pierre Pambrun, had abandoned his two companions to hunt and fish on his own. When he returned, he found a gruesome scene. Only one man was still alive, and that was only because he had eaten the body of his dead companion. Despite the starving man's pleas, Pambrun abandoned him again. Two days later, the second man too was dead.

Rae knew the harshness of the north and what it could force people to do when they were faced with starvation. He felt sympathy for the cannibal and blamed Pambrun for deserting his charges. However, he didn't say anything, because the man sitting across from the fire telling the grim tale was Pambrun himself.

Another Winter of Preparation

British naval officers wrote books about the Arctic too. Often they were based on a few months experience and no knowledge of the background situation. Sometimes they even went as far as criticizing the HBC for its treatment of the First Nations.

Rae, who only ever judged someone on their abilities, never their race or beliefs, was furious. He wrote to Simpson outlining examples of mistreatment carried out by British sailors and officers. He finished by pointing out that the British Government, which knew virtually nothing about conditions in Canada, was complaining about the HBC treatment of the First Nations while allowing tens of thousands of Irish people to die in a potato famine on their own doorstep. Rae was never one to keep quiet when he felt something needed to be said. It was a characteristic that would get him into a lot of trouble.

September 1850 found John Rae back in Fort Confidence preparing one more time to seek out Franklin. It was a mixed winter. Rae was busy with preparations, hunting and HBC business. The last was taking more of his time as Simpson had promoted Rae to Chief Factor in compensation for having to go back to the Arctic.

In January, Rae was pleased to receive a copy of a book he had written, *Narrative of an Expedition to the Shores of the Arctic Sea in 1846 and 1847*. Rae was developing a strong reputation as a competent and efficient Arctic explorer. Almost single-handedly, he had covered more ground in the search for Franklin than any of the large and expensive British Navy expeditions that were busy scouring the Arctic. And he was ready to try again.

The transition to life under European rule was harsh for the First Nations peoples, forcing them, among many other things, to adopt European dress.

Adapting to the Arctic

John Rae was the first European explorer to wear Inuit clothing when travelling. Typically he wore a cloth vest, cloth coat lined with leather and trousers made from moose hide. He wore leather mitts and moccasins large enough to fit blanketing material underneath and edged with fur to keep the snow out. He wore a fur hat and bound his moccasins with leather thongs so that his feet wouldn't slip. His personal possessions were only spare clothes to wear in his snow house, a comb, toothbrush, towel and a piece of soup. This was all much lighter and more efficient than the woollen clothes the Navy continued to wear.

A group of Inuit dressed in the traditional fur clothing that helped them survive where European explorers could not.

1851—On Foot

On 25 April 1851, Rae harnessed dogs, Inuit-style to his sleds, and with four companions headed north. Under the cascading light of the *aurora borealis*, Rae and two companions travelling light and fast, crossed the frozen strait that had defeated him the year before and explored the coast of Victoria Island. Before he returned to the mainland, he had covered over 1500 km of ground, much of it never previously visited by Europeans. It was one of the longest journeys made on foot in the Arctic and yet, at the end of it, Rae was fitter and healthier than he had been in April. He was ready to start the second part of his exploration.

John Rae found no direct indications of Franklin's fate, however, on August 21, he came upon two odd pieces of wood. One was part of a flag staff, and the other was part of an oak ship's stanchion. Both were man-made, and copper tacks in the former carried the mark of the British Government. Rae correctly assumed that the wood had been carried from the north by the ice. But from where? It could have come from a ship in Barrow Strait over 600 km away. In fact, the wood came from either the *Erebus* or the *Terror*, and it had travelled at most 150 km. Franklin and his men had died nearby.

The *aurora borealis*, or northern lights, have fascinated people since the early inhabitants of the North looked skyward. The *aurora* can be bright enough to read a book by. It consists of many forms, from arcs to waving curtains and ranges in colour from greenish blue to purple.

Even today, the lights are poorly understood in detail. They occur when energy from the sun interacts with molecules of oxygen and nitrogen in the high atmosphere around Earth's poles. This causes the molecules to emit radiation, which we see as colour. When solar activity is high, the *aurora* can be seen all over Canada but in the cold silence of an Arctic night, it is an awesome spectacle.

1851—By Boat

John Rae had accomplished much that summer, but he almost accomplished much more. That distant land that he turned his back on was the western shore of King William Island. All along it in 1851 were discarded supplies, abandoned boats, scattered bodies of British sailors and the priceless journals, letters and papers that told the frightful story of the Franklin Expedition's tragic fate. If Rae had made it across Victoria Strait, there would probably have been no mystery surrounding the Franklin disaster. But he didn't, and no one else visited that sad shore for eight more years. By then the bodies were mere skeletons and the papers destroyed. Those years created the Franklin mystery.

In the middle of August, 1851, John Rae stood on the easternmost shore of Victoria Island and and looked across a wide expanse of ice-blocked water. He could see land in the distance and wanted to go there, but three attempts to cross the treacherous ice of Victoria Strait had failed. It was also late in the season, and the journey back was long.

The summer had been a success. Rae had explored much of Victoria Island's previously unknown coast, was the first European to meet the Inuit bands who lived there and discovered that they knew nothing of any lost white men (*kabloonas*). But now it was time to head home. Rae turned his boats south, back to the Coppermine River.

Rae's sketch of Fort Confidence

Home Again

England in 1852 was frantic with worry about the fate of Sir John Franklin. His widow, Lady Jane, was tirelessly lobbying the Navy for more expeditions, and even paying for some out of her own pocket. The public was appalled at the disaster and eager to find out how such a tragedy could have happened. Amidst all this, there were even some who still hoped for the miraculous survival of Franklin or some of his men.

Perhaps the most bizarre of these figures was a retired sea captain, William Coppin. He claimed that in 1849 the ghost of his recently dead daughter had appeared and stated that Franklin and his men were trapped near Victory Point on King William Island. Of course, Franklin and most of his men were dead by this time but, oddly, while experienced Navy men were looking in all the wrong places, the young ghost got the location of the disaster exactly right.

Rae spent the summer of 1852 visiting his ailing mother in Orkney, receiving honours and awards, and making enemies with his outspoken criticism of other failed expeditions. Rae was a hero now, so the enemies didn't matter, but they would come back to haunt him in a few years.

Rae enjoyed his return to the comforts of society and could sometimes be seen strolling through London with an attractive young woman on his arm. But inside he was yearning for the simpler life of the wilderness. In May, he submitted a proposal for a new expedition to complete the mapping of Canada's Arctic coast. In early June he was chosen to lead it.

In November, Rae attended the funeral of the Duke of Wellington, and in March 1853, he boarded a ship bound for New York. His restless spirit had not allowed him a full year at home.

Sir John Franklin

Back to the North

One thing Rae loved about the North was the cleanliness. The crisp, fresh Arctic air was a dramatic contrast to the disgusting stench that rose from the open sewers that still ran through London in the mid 19th century. True, in the Arctic you ran the risk of starving or freezing to death, but in London, cholera, typhus, smallpox and a host of other diseases reduced the average age of death to just 27 years. Half the funerals that rumbled their sombre way through the streets of the capital were of children under ten-years-old. Is it any wonder Rae loved the north?

On May 6 1853, Rae arrived in Sault Ste. Marie on his way north. On the same day he was awarded an honorary degree in medicine from McGill University. The degree was for his exploration and his work with the HBC. It was 20 years since he had qualified as a doctor, and as he noted, "a few questions on medical subjects would have floored me." Also in the Sault, Rae visited his old friend Letitia Hargrave who, unknown to them both, only had a few months left to live.

Rae's journey north was an adventure. On one occasion, a boat was offloading onto an ice floe that broke apart. Until the other boat came to rescue them, Rae and the others stood for half an hour, up to their waists in freezing sea water, battered by waves, with the precious supplies held above their heads.

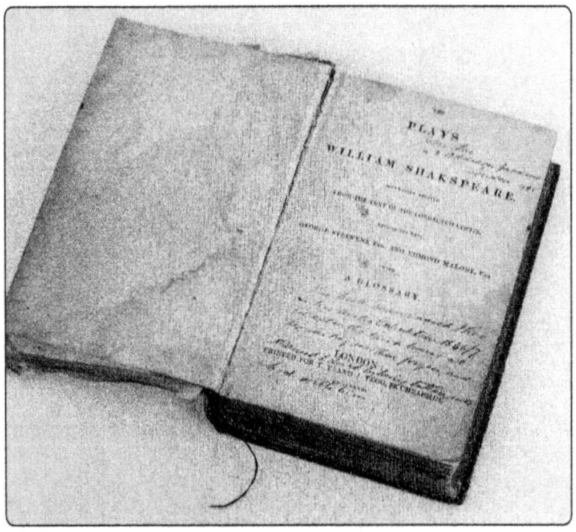

Rae's beloved book of Shakespeare's plays that accompanied him everywhere.

At night, Rae would lie in his tent listening to what sounded like gentle rain on the canvas. But it wasn't rain, it was mosquitoes trying to get in to suck his blood. A swarm of mosquitoes could drive a hardy muskox mad with their bites, so it was a relief when Rae reached Repulse Bay and the weather became too cold for the pests. But Rae's discomfort wasn't over. As the only non-smoker in his party, he had a snow house to himself, but it took several people to warm a snow house, Rae spent an unpleasantly cold winter.

Preparations

Despite the difficulties, there was much work to be done that winter of 1853/54. Food supplies had to be built up through hunting whatever game was around, sledges had to be built and caches of food had to be laid out for the spring explorations. A huge disappointment for Rae was the lack of any sign of Inuit in the area. He had hoped to trade for dogs to pull his sledges. Now he and his men would have to do it themselves.

Man-hauling sledges was slow, gruelling work that could cripple anyone but the fittest. It was vital that Rae reduce their equipment to a minimum.

Planning on a 60 day sledge journey, Rae calculated that he and the four men who would accompany him would need 373 kg of supplies:

177 kg of Pemican,
58 kg of flour,
32 kg of biscuits,
17 kg of preserved potatoes,
18 kg of sugar,
5.5 kg of condensed milk,
61 kg of alcohol for cooking,
2.25 kg of tea and
2.25 kg of chocolate.

Another 80 kg of bedding, guns and ammunition made a total of 453 kg that had to be hauled by five men. Some of this would be placed in caches and picked up on the return journey, but it was still going to be hard work.

Sledge hauling was brutally hard work

The Last Link

John Rae looked at the final link of the Northwest Passage, but he did not sail through it. That honour had to wait for another half century and a Norwegian who had prepared as meticulously and knew as much about Arctic travel as Rae himself.

When he set off to sail through the Northwest Passage in 1903, Roald Amundsen had to do so in the dead of night to avoid creditors. However, Amundsen and his six-man crew were determined to the point of obsession. Despite being beset by ice for two winters in a small cove directly across Rae Strait from where John Rae stood in 1854, Amundsen persevered, and in August 1905, they completed the Northwest Passage for the first time. They had also proved that the strait Rae had seen was indeed the final link in the passage.

On March 31 1854, John Rae set off on his last great journey. He was 40 years old, fit and healthy, and a more experienced Arctic traveller than any other explorer of his time. His goal was to map the last unvisited section of Canada's Arctic coastline and discover the final link in the Northwest Passage.

Rae followed the same route he had taken in 1847, but this time he went further. Despite blizzards, bitter cold and the brutal effort of sledge-hauling, Rae crossed the Boothia Peninsula, reached the furthest east attained by Simpson and Dease in 1839, and mapped north to the furthest west attained by James Clark Ross in 1831. As Rae and his men struggled up the coast of Boothia they could look over a wide expanse of ice to the left. Ice that obviously melted every summer to open a clear channel that would one day be called Rae Strait—the missing piece of the Northwest Passage.

Across the channel, Rae could see land, the east coast of the island whose West Coast he had already seen from Victoria Island in 1851—King William Island. Again, Rae couldn't cross to the island, as it would risk the lives of his men. Rae did not know it, but for the second time in his career, he was looking at the location of the greatest tragedy in the history of Arctic exploration. Satisfied with the geographic discoveries he had made, Rae turned back and began the long march to his camp at Repulse Bay.

Tragedy Discovered

Rae collected a wide variety of relics from the Inuit and brought them back to Britain. They included: broken pieces of guns, watches, compasses and telescopes; a gold watch, medal, spoons and forks belonging to Franklin and several of his officers; and a silver plate engraved, "Sir John Franklin, K.C.E." These, and other sad mementos of tragedy collected by later searchers, are displayed today in museums around Britain and in Canada.

As Rae slogged past Pelly Bay on his way to discovering the Northwest Passage, he met an Inuit wearing a gold cap band. The Inuit said that the band came from a dead *kabloona*, and that he had traded with other Inuit for it. It was not much information to go on, but Rae told the man that he would buy any other relics if they were brought to his camp at Repulse Bay.

After 56 days of gruelling travel, Rae arrived back at Repulse Bay on May 26 1854. There he found several Pelly Bay Inuit eager to trade and tell stories. Rae bought all the relics he could and wrote down all the stories—they were horrific. Four winters before, to the west, some Inuit hunters had met a group of 40 starving *kabloonas* dragging a boat over the ice. The *kabloonas* were led by a tall man with a telescope and they traded for some seal meat before continuing on their journey.

The following spring, the Inuit discovered a camp of tents and an overturned boat. In the tent and underneath the boat were the frozen bodies of at least 30 men. On a nearby island were five more bodies. One of them was a large man who had a telescope strapped to his back.

Rae realized that he was hearing about the tragic fate of Sir John Franklin and his men.

An older Rae showing some of the artifacts he brought back from the Arctic

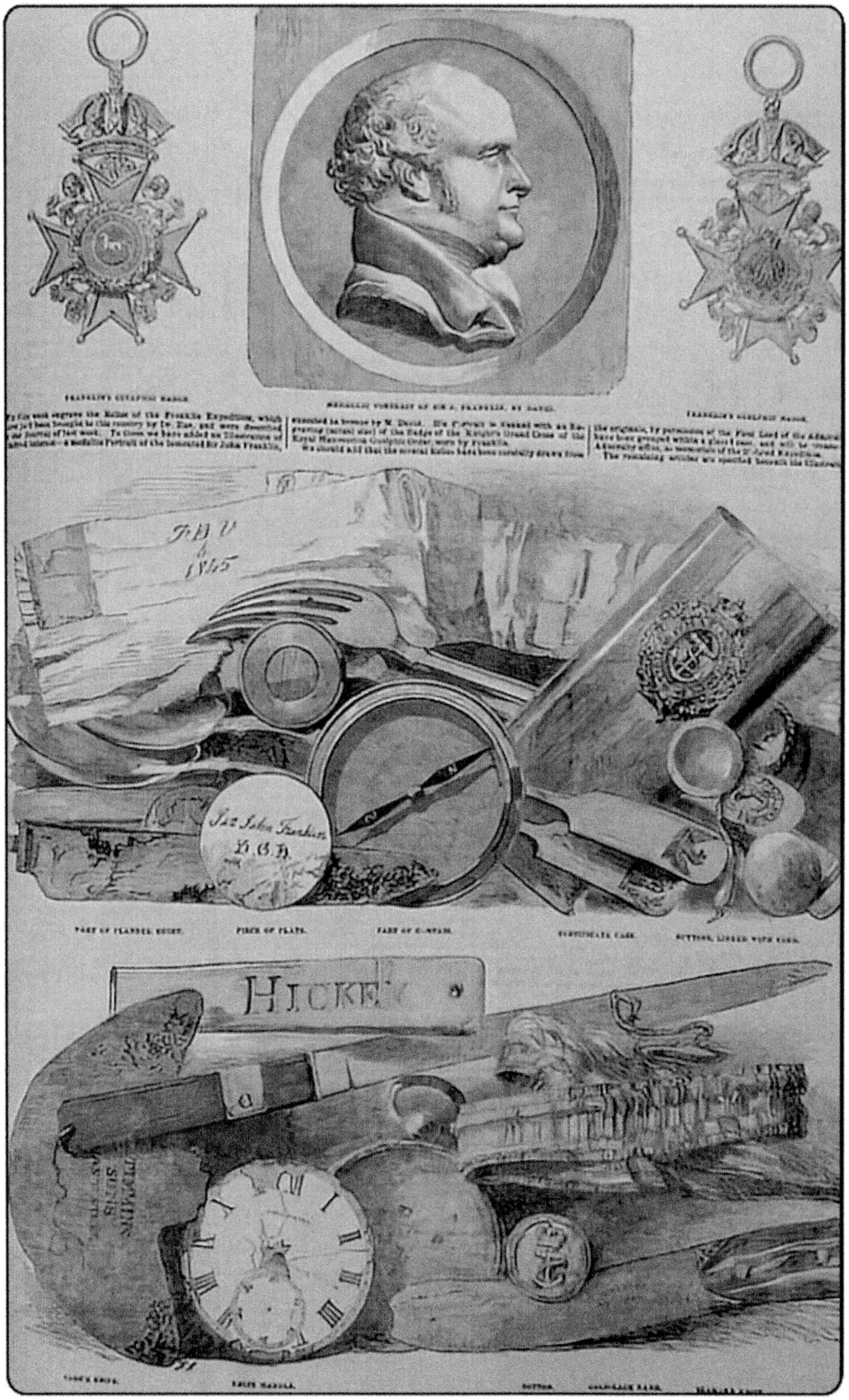

Some of the Franklin artifacts that Rae brought back with him

A Difficult Decision

The storm Rae was unwittingly sailing towards was triggered by one short sentence in the report of his discoveries that he sent on ahead. He talked of something the Inuit had told him about the camp of dead men they had discovered. It read: "From the mutilated state of many of the corpses, and the contents of the kettles, it was evident that our wretched countrymen had been driven to the last resource—cannibalism—as a means of prolonging existence."

As Rae sat in his tent surrounded by the pitiful remnants of the Franklin disaster, he had a tough choice to make. Should he head back to Britain as rapidly as possible to let the waiting world know that he had discovered Franklin's fate, or should he wait another winter in Repulse Bay and visit the site of the tragedy the following spring? Rae chose the former course because others were searching for Franklin far to the north, and he felt a responsibility to get word to them as quickly as possible so that no additional lives would be put at risk.

On August 4 1854, the ice cleared and John Rae sailed from Repulse Bay. On the 21 September, he sailed from York Factory aboard the HBC ship *Prince Rupert*, the vessel that had accompanied him on his first voyage to the wilds of Canada 21 years before. In mid-Atlantic they encountered a violent storm that ripped the sails and nearly washed the lifeboat away. But that was nothing compared to the storm that awaited Rae in London. It would be much worse than anything he had faced in the Arctic wilderness.

A fanciful illustration of the end of Franklin's expedition

A Disappointing Return

The Admiralty had good reasons for publishing Rae's report. They wanted it to be the last word on the Franklin search. Already the government had spent £600,000 (over fifty million Canadian dollars today) on 55 expeditions and now the Crimean War was raging against Russia. All ships were needed. Lady Jane Franklin was noisily arguing for a greater effort to find her husband. In the eyes of the Navy, Rae's report closed the matter—publish it and get on with other things.

On 22 October, Rae was rushed to the Admiralty in London to meet with the First Lord, Sir James Graham. The following day, Rae's report, which he had assumed was confidential, was published in full in the *Times* newspaper, complete with the sentence on cannibalism. Reaction was swift.

Within days, Rae was receiving so many letters that he had to take time off work to reply to them all. Newspapers began to question the report of cannibalism. How could such a "noble band of adventurers" be cannibals? Rae was naive to believe the unsupported stories of "savages". Was it not much more likely that the "Esquimaux" had taken advantage of the sailors' weakened state and murdered them for their equipment?

Perhaps most painful for Rae, he was accused of fabricating in order to claim the £10,000 (close to one million Canadian dollars today) reward for discovering the fate of Franklin. In vain did Rae point out that he could not have been aware of the reward before his return to London, since the *Times* was not available in Repulse Bay. Experienced Arctic explorers, like Rae's friend Dr John Richardson, knew the truth of what Rae was reporting, but they kept silent. Rae's enemies were much too powerful.

In the 19th century, London was the bustling industrial capital of the World

Powerful Enemies

What many of Rae's critics failed to realize was the power of the Inuit stories. The Inuit had no written language and so relied upon stories to preserve their history and culture. That made the stories very important to them, and they preserved them with an accuracy that we find almost unbelievable.

There are cases of stories about Franklin being recorded by different explorers in the 1860s and again in the 1920s. The stories were never written down, they were simply repeated from generation to generation over 60 years. And yet the stories are identical, word for word. If more people had paid attention to the Inuit stories back in the 1850s and 1860s, we would know much more about the fate of Franklin today.

Lady Jane Franklin was an intelligent and powerful woman. While John Franklin was alive, she had manipulated his career shamelessly. She was instrumental in getting him command of his final expedition. Now that he was dead, Jane turned her attention to preserving his memory and turning him into a hero. To do that she enlisted the most famous author of his day, Charles Dickens.

Dickens used his reputation and all his skills as a writer to deny Rae's report and to blame the Inuit for murdering Franklin and his men. It was rubbish, but it was brilliantly written rubbish and Rae had little chance against it.

Rae's reputation was doomed. Even worse, his achievements were questioned.

Charles Dickens, author of *A Christmas Carol, Great Expectations* and many other classics, wrote questioning Rae's evidence

Injustice

Franklin's status as a hero was even expressed in popular songs like *Lord Franklin*:

'Twas late one night in the deep
Swinging in my hammock I fell asleep
I dreamed a dream and I thought it true
Concerning Franklin and his gallant crew

With 100 seamen he sailed away
O'er the frozen ocean in the month of May
To seek a passage around the Pole
Where we poor seamen do sometimes go

Through cruel hardships the sailors rowed
The ships on mountains of ice were thrown
Only the Esquimaux in his skin canoe
Was the only one who ever came through

From Baffin Bay where the whale fishes blow
The fate of Franklin no man may know
The fate of Franklin no tongue can tell
Lord Franklin among his sailors do dwell

And now my burden it brings me pain
My long-lost Franklin I would cross the main
Ten thousand pounds would I freely give
To say on Earth that Lord Franklin did live

After Francis McClintock returned in 1859 from visiting the place Rae had identified as the site of Franklins' end, Jane Franklin decided to promote her dead husband as the discoverer of the Northwest Passage. An officer called McClure had already claimed the prize, although he had walked most of the passage on ice that no sailing ship could ever get through. But to Jane it was history that mattered. Until her death in 1875, she strove tirelessly to turn her husband into a hero, and it worked. Franklin is commemorated on countless monuments and books as the discoverer of the Northwest Passage. Franklin failed and became a hero—Rae succeeded and was ignored.

McClintock's men discovering the remains of two of Franklin's men

The Northwest Passage Stolen

McLure, who walked through the Northwest Passage

When John Rae stood on the shores of Rae Strait in 1854, he was looking at the only possible Northwest Passage navigable to sailing ships. In fact, it may have been a route that Franklin tried in 1846, and failed because his ships had too deep a draught for the shallow waters of Rae Strait. It was only in the middle of the 20th century, almost 100 years after Rae, that powerful ships' engines enabled them to force a way through the dreadful pack ice that Franklin was forced into. Until then, the only passage was the one mapped by the HBC men, Simpson and Dease and John Rae. That was hard for the British Navy to accept—they had spent all the money, and they had suffered all the disasters. Now they wanted all the credit.

As Rae's reputation was being systematically destroyed, a new Arctic map was published by the Navy. It showed Rae's discoveries, but the note said that they were the work of Collinson, a naval captain who had sailed that way two years after Rae. Rae complained and the note was changed, but it still gave no mention of Rae. It was hard for the Navy to admit that an HBC man was a more efficient and more clever traveller than their officers.

One Last Attempt

It is fascinating to wonder what might have happened had the *Iceberg* not sunk. Rae's skills, his plans, and even his boat, were very similar to those that Roald Amundsen had at his disposal when he eventually sailed the Passage in 1905. Given the chance, Rae might well have succeeded 47 years earlier. Not even Jane Franklin could then have denied him the recognition he deserved.

Despite his stated desire to settle with a wife and family in Britain, Rae could not let the Arctic go. Perhaps it seemed a simpler place after his experiences with Franklin's widow. In any case, in April 1856, Rae resigned from the HBC after 23 years of service. He moved to Hamilton, Ontario, where his brothers still lived and made a plan to sail the Northwest Passage.

Using some of the money he had finally been awarded for discovering Franklin's fate, he built a schooner called the *Iceberg*. Delays meant that the ship was not finished in time for the 1857 season, so he gave the vessel to his brothers to use on the Great Lakes trade over the winter. Unfortunately, she sank in a storm in the autumn, ending Rae's dream.

Roald Amundsen

Falling in Love at Last

Perhaps some of Kate's father's reticence stemmed from Rae's eccentricities. Never one to worry too much about what others thought of him, Rae sometimes appeared on the street in Inuit clothes. His speech was peppered with Inuit words that no one else could understand, and he would sometimes, without warning, shout commands to imaginary teams of huskies. To a military man like Major Thompson, this must have been very worrisome, and it is to his credit that he did eventually allow his precious daughter to marry the rather odd man she fell in love with.

In 1858, at a service in a Toronto cathedral, John Rae met Catherine Jane Alicia Thompson and fell head over heels in love. It didn't matter that he was 46 and she only 21 or that Kate's father disapproved. Little would stop Rae once his mind was made up.

In the autumn, Rae was at Fort Garry on a hunting trip with Sir George Simpson and two other men. A letter arrived from Kate saying that her father had forbidden any marriage because he believed that Rae probably had several native wives and children already.

Immediately, Rae abandoned the hunting trip and rushed back to Hamilton. There his old friend James Hargrave, Letitia's widower, vouched for Rae's character, and Kate's father reluctantly agreed. John and Kate were married in Toronto in January 1860.

Catherine (Kate) Thompson

Still a Traveller

Although just married, Rae was in no mood to settle down. Immediately after the wedding, the newlyweds sailed for Britain, where they would make their home. But Rae was still restless. His first summer of married life, he left Kate to survey the Faroe Islands, Iceland and Greenland for a telegraph route. Then, in 1861, he brought Kate back to Canada. While she visited her family in Hamilton, John led a hunting trip out west.

The party travelled along the Assiniboine and Qu'Appelle Rivers and were the first Europeans to map Chaplin and Old Wives Lakes near present-day Regina. Only the presence ahead of threatening First Nations prevented a longer journey.

In 1861, travelling in western Canada was not as taxing as the Arctic Rae was used to, but it was still no easy matter. After leaving the settlements along the Red River, everything to the west was wild. Either you had to carry your own food or hunt. Travel was by horseback or ox-cart, and you either suffocated in a hot, dry cloud of dust or were bogged down in a quagmire of mud.

The experienced Rae and his party had no problems. They travelled light, fast and comfortably. Thirteen years later, the 300 untrained men of the fledgling North West Mounted Police struggled for four months across the same land, almost starving, and leaving a trail of dead oxen and horses in their wake. People were still not ready to learn from Rae.

A squad of the pioneering North West Mounted Police

Across Canada

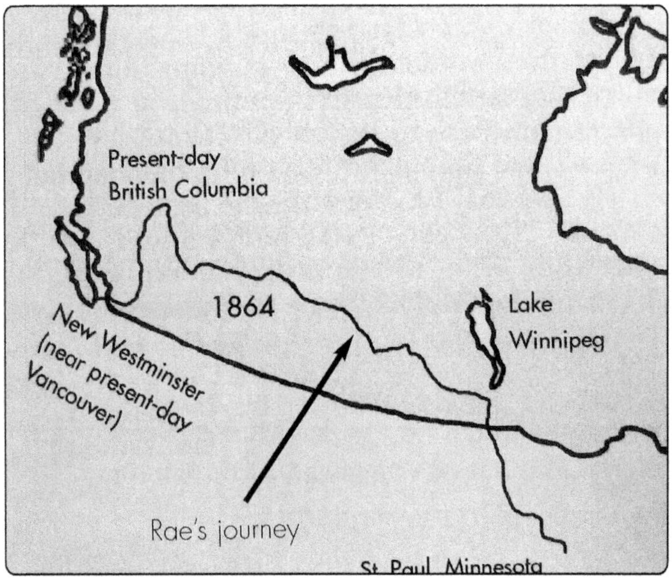

In 1864, Rae undertook to survey a telegraph route across Canada to the Pacific Coast. Not wanting to be left behind again, Kate accompanied John as far as Fort Garry in Manitoba before turning back for home in Britain.

Rae had not lost his touch. He could still walk more than 30 km a day and canoe the treacherous rapids of the Fraser River in a dugout canoe. From Victoria, British Columbia, Rae caught a steamer to Panama in Central America, crossed the isthmus by train and took a boat for Britain. Kate who had taken the direct route back, did not beat him by very much. At 50 years old, John Rae still made travelling look easy.

Home at Last

In 1865, John and Kate rented Berstane House, a waterfront estate outside Kirkwall on Orkney. Sleeping in a comfortable bed every night and eating as much as he wanted with cutlery off a linen tablecloth were pleasant novelties for John, but he and Kate were not content. They had no children and, much as they enjoy the rugged wilds of Orkney, they missed the intellectual bustle of the city. In 1869 they moved to London where John lived for the rest of his life.

Even 15 years after Rae's report on Franklin's fate was published, Jane Franklin still thirsted for revenge. In 1869, Sofia Cracroft, Franklin's niece and Jane's constant companion, wrote to Rae accusing him of writing an anonymous letter to Lady Franklin and charged him with being disrespectful to the explorer and stealing the relics of the expedition.

Rae replied calmly that he had not written the letter, that while Franklin was not "a good walker", he had never been disrespectful and that he had purchased the relics from the Inuit and showed them to thousands of people, hardly the activities of a thief. He concluded that he was "perfectly indifferent" to what Cracroft did with the anonymous letter. This appears to have ended the matter.

John and Kate

Retirement

At 73 years old, Rae decided to attend his volunteer regiment's review at Dover. Rising at three in the morning, he walked six km to the train in less than an hour; travelled for 2 1/2 hours; spent 10 hours walking, running, shooting, climbing and marching; travelled back on the train; and only got a carriage home because he did not want to keep Kate up late.

Retirement did not prevent John Rae from doing things. He wrote papers on scientific topics ranging from icebergs and glaciers to intelligence in animals and duck diving. He regarded the achievements of the Inuit in snow house building, harpoon manufacture and snow goggles as highly developed technology rather than the quaint ingenuity that most of his contemporaries thought it. He toured the country speaking to learned audiences in Oxford, Edinburgh, Dublin and, in 1882, Montreal.

He never shrank from controversy, loudly criticizing the Nares Arctic Expedition of 1875 for making many of the mistakes Franklin had made and not learning from private expeditions such as his own. He championed the use of men familiar with conditions and hunting in the Arctic over well-disciplined but unimaginative and poorly-trained sailors. As late as 1891, he was still writing letters to have his discoveries acknowledged on the Admiralty charts. In order to keep fit, Rae volunteered in the London Scottish Regiment, marching, exercising and shooting with the best of the much younger men. John Rae was getting older, but he was not going to give into it.

Rest

At seven in the evening, during a beautiful sunset on 22 July, 1893, after 79 years of life, 33 of them happily married to Kate, John Rae died of an aneurysm at his home in London.

Kate took her husband's body back to his beloved Orkney, where he was buried behind Saint Magnus Cathedral in Kirkwall. Then she journeyed back south. It would be 26 years before she followed him.

There is a statue of John Rae in St. Magnus Cathedral. He lies asleep beneath a buffalo robe, with his book of Shakespeare and his musket beside him. The sculpture was paid for by local citizens and the inscription says

'John Rae, M.D., L.L.D, F.R.S, F.R.G.S.
Arctic Explorer
Intrepid discoverer of the fate of Sir John Franklin's last expedition
Born 1813—died 1893
Expeditions: 1846-7, 1848-9, 1851-2, 1853-4.
Erected by public subscription. 1895.'

It is good that John Rae is remembered, but it would be better if he were remembered more for his achievements rather than his relationship with those of Franklin.

Rae's statue in St. Magnus Cathedral

Remembered

One of the best tributes to John Rae was written by Viljalmur Stefansson who, early in the 20th century, spent many years living in the Arctic with the Inuit. In comparing Rae to the official naval expeditions of the time which caused "much needless suffering" and "deplorable tragedies", through their inflexibility and incompetence, Stefansson called Rae, "a man exact and truthful and in his methods of travel a generation ahead of his time...he...put into effect the only sound principle of the traveller—that of doing in Rome as the Romans do."

Between 1846 and 1854, John Rae led four major explorations, travelling 40,000 km, almost 3000 of them previously unexplored. He was generations ahead of his time in adopting Inuit methods of travel, living and hunting. Only one man died on any of his expeditions, and none suffered anything like the horrors that accompanied even successful British Naval expeditions of the same time. Rae was remarkably free from the prejudices of his day, admiring skill regardless of whether it was shown by an Orcadian, Métis or Inuit.

John Rae's problem was that he was strong-minded, intelligent and efficient, not qualities that were necessarily valued highly in the 1850s. Added to that, he was outspoken in favour of what he saw as fairness, truth and justice. That is what made him powerful enemies, destroyed his reputation and denied him the honours he deserved.

All of Rae's discoveries, including the presence of cannibalism amongst the last of Franklin's men, have been subsequently proven correct. But sometimes being right in the wrong way carries a price. Rae was one of the greatest of the 19th century Arctic explorers, yet he was the only one never to be knighted.

Rae's Life and Times

September 30, 1813	John Rae is born in Orkney, Scotland.
1814	Sir Walter Scott visits the Rae's.
1819	John Rae's father represents HBC in Orkney.
1827	William Rae leaves for Rupert's Land.
1829	John Rae attends the Royal College of Surgeons (RCS) in Edinburgh.
1830	Richard Rae leaves for Rupert's Land.
1833	In April, Rae graduates from the RCS before sailing to Rupert's Land aboard the *Prince of Wales*.
	John Rae arrives at Moose Factory.
September 1833	Winter on Charlton Island in Hudson Bay.
1833/4	Rae returns to Moose Factory and takes up the post
Summer of 1834	of surgeon.
	Rae travels to Ottawa and Montreal and plans an
1843/4	Arctic expedition.
	Sir John Franklin sets off from London to sail
May 1845	through the Northwest Passage.
	Rae meets the author Robert Ballantyne.
September 1845	Rae sails north from York Factory.
13 June, 1846	Rae overwinters in Repulse Bay and explores the
1846/7	shores of Boothia and the Melville Peninsula.
	Rae sails for London.
September 1847	Rae and John Richardson search the Arctic coast
1848	between the McKenzie and Coppermine Rivers for signs of Franklin.
	Rae fails to cross Dolphin and Union Strait to
1849	Victoria Island. Albert One-Eye dies on return journey.

1851	Rae explores the coast of Victoria Island and finds fragments of wood from Franklin's ships.
March 1852	Rae returns to London.
1853	Rae returns to York Factory and sets out north once more.
August 1853	Rae returns to Repulse Bay and prepares to overwinter.
Summer 1854	Rae crosses Boothia Peninsula and looks over the last link in the Northwest Passage. On his return to Repulse Bay, Rae hears the first concrete news of Franklin's fate and collects relics from the Inuit.
October 1854	Rae returns to England to be greeted with horror at his report of cannibalism amongst the last survivors of Franklin's men.
December 1854	Charles Dickens publishes and angry rebuttal of Rae's report.
April 1856	Rae resigns from the Hudson Bay Company.
June 1856	Rae is finally paid the ten thousand pound reward for discovering Franklin's fate.
Summer, 1859	Leopold McClintock's expedition finds bones, abandoned supplies and a note on King William Island, confirming Rae's report.
1857/9	John Rae lives with his brothers in Hamilton, Ontario.
January 1860	Rae marries Catherine Thompson.
1861	Rae leads a hunting expedition to Western Canada.
1864	Rae leads a survey party for a telegraph line across Canada.
1865/7	Rae lives in Orkney before moving to London.
1882	Rae visits Canada for the last time.
July 22, 1893	John Rae dies and is buried at St. Magnus Cathedral in Kirkwall on Orkney.

Acknowledgements

Firstly, thanks must go to Sylvia McConnell who did such a wonderful job with Napoleon Publishing and who gave many of my early efforts, including this book and my very first novel, a chance to see the light of day. Also to Allister Thompson, Napoleon's editor and map creator who, incidentally, impressed the hell out of my son by once touring as the supporting act for Alice Cooper.

Secondly, this new edition is richer for Liz Milkau's kindness in allowing me to use her original illustrations for no return other than the glory—thank you.

And finally, thanks go to Fiona Gould of the John Rae Society on Orkney who triggered the idea for this new edition and whose eagle editorial eye has spotted numerous occasions where my dictation software has been confused by my Scottish accent.

Photo Credits

National Archives of Canada
Pages 2, 10, 14, 17, 23, 24, 25, 27, 28, 29, 35, 36, 39, 40, 43, 45, 53, 55, 57, 58, 63, 65

Orkney Library Photographic Archive
Pages 4, 5, 6,8, 67, 69.

Hudson's Bay Company Archives, Provincial Archives of Manitoba
Pages 15, 34, 41, 50, 62, 64

Archives of Ontario
Pages 22, 47, 48.

The Trustees of the National Museums of Scotland
Pages 42, 52.

Library of Congress
Pages 60.

Cover background is a detail of *Aurora Borealis* by Frederic Edwin Church, 1865
Photograph of John Rae's statue in Stromness, courtesy of James Grieve.

The John Rae Society

The John Rae Society was formed in 2013 and has grown to a membership of over 400 members on three continents. The society has three main aims: to obtain for John Rae the recognition he deserves; to establish an Arctic centre in his honour at his childhood home; and to preserve and restore the Hall of Clestrain to its former splendour.

To date, the society and its enthusiastic membership have raised sufficient funds to purchase the Hall and land for an access road. They have also carried out roof and floor repairs to protect the Hall from further deterioration. Surveys, design and business plans have all been completed, despite delays due to the recent pandemic.

Built in 1769, the Hall of Clestrain holds a unique position in Orkney's architectural heritage. In addition to being the Rae family home, it has been the seat of the Laird and a working farm. It was abandoned to the elements after suffering severe damage in the great storm of 1952, but it is hoped that one day the Hall will be restored to the splendour that once rivalled the impressive villas in far away Edinburgh.

For further information please visit the website: www.johnraesociety.com where you will find updates on the progress of the project, as well as details of how to join the Society or make donations.

The Hall of Clestrain as it may have looked in its heyday.

Drawing by Iris Heddle, courtesy of Orcadian Ltd, Kirkwall Orkney UK.

Other Titles by the Author

John Franklin: A Brief Biography

Sir John Franklin was many things in his life: an officer in the great naval battles of Copenhagen and Trafalgar; governor of Van Diemen's Land; an explorer from Australia to the Arctic, but it is for his mysterious death and the deaths of all 128 of his crew that he is remembered today. The mystery of the disappearance of the Franklin Expedition to the Northwest Passage has captivated thousands in the 174 years since his men buried Franklin in an unknown grave in the frozen land that kept calling him back. For most of that time only a handful of graves, scattered bones, fragments of debris and Inuit stories have fuelled the speculation as to what killed them all. Now, the wrecks of both of Franklin's ships have been found, preserved in the frigid waters off King William Island, and may contain answers that have been sought for generations. This is the story of the man whose name will forever be associated with the greatest tragedy in Arctic exploration history.

"This book, admirable in its succinctness…is the best life of Franklin yet produced… there could be no better introduction to the life and journeys of Franklin than Wilson's… wonderfully engaging book."—Russell Potter, Arctic Book Review

An *"…excellent overview, the reader is left with an appreciation of the enormous task early exploration of the Arctic represented…a first rate story and a very useful addition to our understanding and appreciation of an important and unique segment of Canadian history. Highly Recommended."*—CM Magazine

The Alchemist's Dream

In the fall of 1669, the Nonsuch returns to London with a load of fur from Hudson Bay. It brings something else, too—the lost journal from Henry Hudson's tragic search for a passage to Cathay in 1611. In the hands of a greedy sailor, the journal is merely an object to sell. But for Robert Bylot—a once-great maritime explorer—the book is a painful reminder of a past he'd rather forget. As Bylot relives his memories of a plague-ridden city, of the mysterious alchemist John Dee, and of mutiny in the frozen wastes of Hudson Bay, an age-old mystery is both revealed and solved. Set against the thrilling backdrop of the quest for the Northwest Passage, The Alchemist's Dream is a riveting tale of exploration, ambition, and betrayal. Also available in an expanded edition that includes extracts from Hudson's journal, **The Final Alchemy**.

"In this engrossing historical adventure, John Wilson paints a vivid picture of a bygone era involving Henry Hudson's fateful search for the elusive Northwest Passage, an

alchemist, mysterious passengers, and enigmatic maps. The Alchemist's Dream fascinates from start to finish."—Governor General's Award jury citation.

Graves of Ice

Thrilled at being a part of such a great adventure, George Chambers volunteers to join Sir John Franklin's expedition in search of the elusive Northwest Passage. But as the ice traps both *Erebus* and *Terror* in a desolate, frozen landscape, the explorers' search for the fabled passage deteriorates to a grim struggle to avoid death by starvation, freezing or scurvy. Eventually, only George remains alive searching vainly for a rescuing sail on the horizon.

"...a compelling story...a haunting story that keeps the reader riveted." CM Magazine

Shot at Dawn

Allan McBride has fought in some of the First World War's bloodiest battles. He has seen his comrades, and his best friend, killed. But tonight he waits in a shed outside Amiens, accused of desertion, to discover if dawn will bring a last-minute reprieve—or execution by firing squad.

"...the powerful writing and strong characters will grip readers from beginning to end." —Quill & Quire

Lost Cause *(The SEVEN Series)*

Steve travels to Spain and uncovers his late grandfather's involvement in the Spanish Civil War. Followed by a sequel, **Broken Arrow** and a prequel, **The Missing Skull**

"I had to force myself to take a break for food and sleep. I just wanted to keep reading." —ALSA's Top Ten review program

And in the Morning: Somme 1916

"And in the Morning joins other outstanding novels about the First World War—an invaluable resource for libraries and classrooms."—Jeffrey Canton, Quill & Quire

Four Steps to Death: Stalingrad 1942

"This absorbing, well-crafted tale...is a haunting description of the tragedy and irony of war...In this vivid narrative, the awful cacophony of war comes to life...the skilled author succeeds without moralistic preaching in highlighting the harsh reality, the utter misery, and the heartbreak of war in this intricate but fascinating book."—VOYA

Lost in Spain: The Spanish Civil War 1936

"Wilson offers a unique perspective on this fascinating era...even minor characters are brought to life."—Library Journal

Flags of War: Shiloh 1862

"...action-filled, tightly written prose. Realistic battle scenes illustrate the senselessness of war...the story offers a fresh take on the conflict - the idea of Canada as refuge for fugitive slaves and the irony of how it was nearly drawn into the war on the side of the South."—Albany Public Library, NY

Battle Scars: Libby Prison 1865
"Readable and exciting."—Booklist

Germania: The Roman Empire 9 A.D.
"This riveting, haunting tale will leave readers clamouring for more."—Best Books

Where Soldiers Lie: India 1857
"This is an absolutely terrific book...Never lagging with a credible hero and an exotic setting...The pacing is flawless."—Geoffrey Bilson Award for Historical Fiction Jury Citation
"The tension and action of the battle and the intense danger of the escape from the massacre will keep readers turning these pages."—Quill & Quire

A Soldier's Sketchbook: The Illustrated First World War Diary of R. H. Rabjohn
A unique First World War diary, illustrated with more than a hundred stunning pencil and ink sketches, for children learning history and also for adults interested in a new perspective on the war and authentic wartime artefacts.
"*The extracts from the diary describe intimate wartime experiences of death and destruction in gruesomely dispassionate terms...it's a story of unmitigated horror, highlighting more than any textbook the futility of war...This unique compilation of firsthand impressions of the Great War will be a valuable resource for adults and teens with an interest in this turning point in world history.*"—Kirkus Starred Review
"The excellent and succinct text . . . provides context for Rabjohn's short diary entries, many of which merely scratch the surface of the suffering he experienced during his time at war."—Starred Review, Quill & Quire

Norman Bethune: A Brief Biography
As a young man, Norman Bethune served as a stretcher-bearer in the First World War. The experience left him with the dedication and passion to lead crusades to find a cure for tuberculosis, to introduce universal health care in Canada, and to introduce mobile blood transfusion units to save wounded soldier's lives on the battlefield. He served with the Republican armies during the Spanish Civil War and in China where he died of blood poisoning in 1939. Because of his left wing politics, Bethune was ignored for decades in his home country. His childhood home in Gravenhurst, Ontario sees large numbers of visitors each year, although a majority are tourists from China where he is revered as a

hero for his work with Mao's army in its fight against the Japanese. Regardless of politics, Bethune deserves to be more highly regarded everywhere for his lifelong struggle against injustice and suffering wherever he encountered it.
"I couldn't put the Bethune story down...It is an inspirational tale as well as a historically important one."—Times-Colonist
"...John Wilson makes the private man come alive...[a] gripping story of a larger-than-life Canadian hero."—Quill & Quire

Heretic: The Heretic's Secret book 1
The Heretic's Secret Trilogy is a rollicking historical adventure set during the bloody 13th century wars against the Cathar Heretics of Languedoc. When the armoured knights of Pope Innocent III swept south in 1209, most thought they would be gone by summer's end but, led by the fanatical Arnaud Aumery and the ambitious Simon de Montfort, they stayed for three fiery decades.
John and Peter enjoy arguing about their differing views of the world. Peter sees the Church and an unquestioning acceptance of God's word as the way to salvation. John sees developing an understanding of the wonder of the world around him as a way of becoming closer to God. As the chaos of war erupts around them, the friendly differences of childhood demand that they take sides. Troubled by mysterious visions, Peter seeks refuge in the Church and becomes an assistant to the militant Aumery. Repelled by the horror he sees around him, John finds himself drawing closer to the persecuted Cathar heretics. As the flames of the Inquisition spread, Peter and John find themselves on opposite sides of a dangerous search for a secret that may have the power to change the world. **Quest** and **Rebirth** follow John and Peter's thrilling adventures to their heart-rending conclusion.
"...a brave book, an unsettling book, and one that is very much needed at this time."—The Globe and Mail
"...an astonishingly nuanced and masterfully told story..."—Quill & Quire

Find out more about these and other titles by John Wilson at www.johnwilson.com. All of John's 50 books are available through Amazon.

Printed in Great Britain
by Amazon

84668941R00052